# PROBLEM SOLVING
## Step-by-Step

**Metropolitan Teaching and Learning Company**
33 Irving Place
New York, New York 10003

Printed in the United States of America

ISBN: 1-58120-703-4

# STEP 3 • Table of Contents

# STEP 3 • Topics

## Tables

## Pictographs

## Bar Graphs

## Other Visual Displays

## Multi-Step Problems

## Recognizing Important Information

## Visual Thinking

## Answer Interpretation

## Categorizing

## Algebraic Thinking

# Using a Table

To solve a math problem, you may need to get information from a table.

**A.** The title of the table tells you what it is about.
**What is this table about?** Ring one.

| Money in Our Pockets | |
| --- | --- |
| Name | Money |
| Ben | 7¢ |
| Jill | 2¢ |
| Karen | 9¢ |
| Louis | 8¢ |

- (how much money different people have)

- how many people have money

**B.** Columns go up and down. The label at the top of the column tells you what information is in that column. The names of the people are in the column on the left.

**What information is in the column on the right?**

amount of money

**C.** Rows go across. Find the name "Ben" in the **Name** column. Read across the row to the **Money** column.

**What amount of money is in this column?**  7¢

So, Ben has 7¢ in his pocket.

**D.** You can use the table to solve an addition problem.

**Example:** How much money do Karen and Jill have together?

**Step 1:** Read the table.

**How much money does Karen have?**  9¢

**How much money does Jill have?**  2¢.

**Step 2:** Write and solve an addition sentence.  9 + 2 = 11

**Answer the question:** Together Karen and Jill have  11¢.

© 1999 Metropolitan Teaching & Learning Co.

● Basic Addition Facts

## GUIDED PRACTICE

Use the table from page 5, and the information in the picture, to solve the problems.

1. Louis and Ben put their money together. Can they buy the paintbrush?

   **Step 1:** Read the table. **How much money does Louis have?**

   _____

   **How much money does Ben have?**

   _____

   **Step 2: Write and solve an addition sentence.**

   _____  Together, they have _____.

   **Step 3:** Look at the picture to find out how much the paintbrush costs.

   Compare the money they have with the cost of the paintbrush. **Ring one.**

   15¢ is more than 16¢        15¢ is less than 16¢

   **Answer the question:** _____

   whistle – 15¢

   top – 10¢

   pencil – 17¢

   paintbrush – 16¢

   eraser – 11¢

   beaded bracelet – 9¢

2. Which two students can put their money together to buy the pencil?

   **Step 1:** Look at the picture. The pencil costs _____.

   **Step 2:** Add pairs of numbers on the table.

   **What two numbers on the table have a sum of 17?**

   _____

   **Step 3:** Read the table.

   **Who has 9¢?** _____

   **Who has 8¢?** _____

   **Answer the question:** _____

## PRACTICE

Use the information in the table to solve the problems.

1. What does the column on the left tell you?

   _____

2. What does the column on the right tell you?

   _____

   _____

| Color Tiles in the Box | |
| --- | --- |
| Color | Number of Tiles |
| Purple | 7 |
| Blue | 6 |
| Yellow | 5 |
| Green | 6 |
| Pink | 4 |
| Red | 9 |
| Brown | 3 |
| Orange | 9 |

3. Jessalyn put all the pink and red tiles in a row. How many tiles did she use?

   Jessalyn used _____.

4. Keenan put all the blue and purple tiles in a pile. How many tiles did he use?

   Keenan used _____.

5. Keisha showed Tom how to make the letter A using all the yellow and blue tiles. How many tiles did she use?

   Keisha used _____.

6. Roger made a design using all the green and purple tiles. How many tiles were in his design?

   Roger's design had

   _____.

7. Dawn wants to make a design that uses 12 tiles. Can she make the design using all the blue and green tiles?

   _____

# TEST-TAKING PRACTICE

Choose the best answer for each problem.

| Animals Treated at Clinic | |
|---|---|
| Animal | Number |
| Birds | 3 |
| Cats | 7 |
| Small Dogs | 9 |
| Large Dogs | 6 |
| Fish | 4 |
| Snakes | 2 |
| Mice | 1 |

**1. How many birds were treated at the clinic?**

**A** 2     **C** 7

**B** 3     **D** 9

**2. How many dogs in all did the clinic treat?**

**J** 6     **L** 15

**K** 9     **M** 16

**3. Some of the animals treated do not have feet. How many animals without feet were treated at the clinic?**

**A** 1     **C** 4

**B** 2     **D** 6

**4. One animal doctor saw only two kinds of animals. She saw 4 animals in all. Which two kinds of animals did she see?**

**J** cats and small dogs

**K** fish and mice

**L** snakes and mice

**M** birds and mice

**5. Another animal doctor treated all the large dogs and all the fish. How many animals did he treat?**

**A** 6     **C** 12

**B** 10     **D** 16

## Write About It

**6. How would you figure out how many cats were treated at the clinic?**

_____

_____

1. A ☐   B ☐   C ☐   D ☐     4. J ☐   K ☐   L ☐   M ☐

2. J ☐   K ☐   L ☐   M ☐     5. A ☐   B ☐   C ☐   D ☐

3. A ☐   B ☐   C ☐   D ☐

● Basic Addition Facts

# Deciding What to Do First

Sometimes you have to find the sum of three numbers to solve a problem. First choose two numbers that you can add easily.

**Example 1:** Gina counts birds in a park. She counts 4 birds in trees, 6 birds on the ground, and 5 birds on a bush. How many birds does she count?

**A.** First, look for two numbers you can add easily.

**Are there doubles?** __no__ **Can you make a ten?** __yes__

**B.** First make the ten.        Then finish adding.

$$\begin{matrix} 4 \\ 6 \end{matrix} \Big\rangle 10$$
$$+\ 5$$

$$\begin{array}{r} 10 \\ +\ 5 \\ \hline 15 \end{array}$$

**Answer the question:** Gina counts ___15 birds___

**Example 2:** Tom saw 4 robins in the morning and 3 robins at noon. Then he saw 4 robins in the afternoon. How many robins did he see?

**Step 1:** First, look for two numbers you can add easily. You can use a double to solve this problem.

**Step 2:** First find a double.        Then finish adding.

$$\begin{matrix} 4 \\ 3 \end{matrix} \Big\rangle 8$$
$$+\ 4$$

$$\begin{array}{r} 8 \\ +\ 3 \\ \hline 11 \end{array}$$

**Answer the question:** Tom saw ___11 robins___.

# GUIDED PRACTICE

First, find the numbers you can add easily.

**1.** Alice had 3 dimes. Her mother gives her 6 dimes. Then she finds 3 dimes. How many dimes does Alice have now?

**Step 1:** Write the numbers you will add.

**Step 2:** Choose two numbers to add first. Look for numbers that are doubles or that make a ten. Find the sum of the numbers you chose.

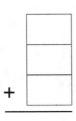   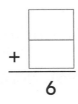   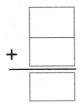   

+ ___          + 6          + ___

**Step 3:** Finish adding.

**Answer the question:** Alice has _____ dimes.

**2.** Jeremy had 5¢ in his pockets. He found 2¢ on the sidewalk and 8¢ on his dresser. How much money does Jeremy have?

**Step 1:** Set up the addition problem.

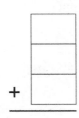      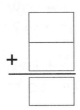   

+ ___          + ___          + ___

**Step 2:** Find the easiest sum. Then finish adding.

**Answer the question:** Jeremy has _____

## PRACTICE

Do the easiest sum first. Show your work.

1. Dana counts 2 orange butterflies, 8 yellow butterflies, and 4 black butterflies. How many butterflies does she count?

   _____

2. John has 2 pennies in his pocket and 2 pennies in his hand. He has 9 pennies at home. How many pennies does he have?

   _____

3. In a kennel there are 3 brown dogs, 7 black dogs, and 8 spotted dogs. How many dogs are in the kennel?

   _____

4. A beekeeper saw 6 bees on a flower. He saw 6 bees in a hive, and 7 bees flying. How many bees did he see?

   _____

5. Carl bought paint for 5 dollars. He bought a paintbrush for 3 dollars and art paper for 5 dollars. How much did Carl spend?

   _____

6. Pedro plays soccer. In one game he scored 4 goals. In another game he scored 6 goals. In the last game he scored 2 goals. How many goals did Pedro score?

   _____

● Adding Three Numbers

# TEST-TAKING PRACTICE

Choose the best answer for each problem.

**1.** Leetha plays softball. She scored 4 runs in one game and 8 runs in another game. She scored 2 runs in a third game. How many runs did Leetha score?

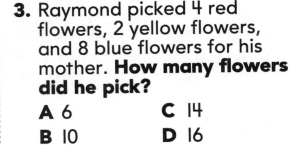

**What is the first step you would take to find the answer?**

**A** Make a ten.
**B** Find a double.
**C** Add 4 + 8.
**D** Find the sum of 4 + 8 + 2.

**2. 5 + 6 + 5 is the same as**

**J** 5 + 6      **L** 10 + 6
**K** 10 + 5     **M** 10 + 16

**3.** Raymond picked 4 red flowers, 2 yellow flowers, and 8 blue flowers for his mother. **How many flowers did he pick?**

**A** 6      **C** 14
**B** 10     **D** 16

**4.** Jesse buys a movie ticket for 6 dollars. He spends 2 dollars on a drink and then buys a poster for 6 dollars. **How much money does he spend?**

**J** 6 dollars
**K** 8 dollars
**L** 12 dollars
**M** 14 dollars

## Write About It

**5.** How does knowing how to find a sum of ten help you to add three numbers?

_____

_____

_____

1. A ☐  B ☐  C ☐  D ☐      3. A ☐  B ☐  C ☐  D ☐
2. J ☐  K ☐  L ☐  M ☐      4. J ☐  K ☐  L ☐  M ☐

● Adding Three Numbers

# Using a Picture

Sometimes you can draw a picture to help you solve
a problem.

**Example:** Kevin has 7 star erasers. The rest of his erasers
are animals. In all, he has 13 erasers. How many animal erasers
does Kevin have?

**A.** You know one part of the sum and you know the sum.

**Write a word sentence to show the problem.**

7 erasers + 7 erasers = 13 erasers

**B.** Make a picture to show Kevin's erasers.

**Draw the part you know.**          **Draw more erasers until
                                      you have 13.**

7 star erasers                        This is the missing part.

13 erasers in all

**C. Write a number sentence to show the problem.**

7 + 6 = 13

**Answer the question:** Kevin has ___6___ animal erasers.

## GUIDED PRACTICE

1. Beth has 7 postcards from California. She has 11 postcards in all. How many of her postcards are *not* from California?

   **Step 1:** You know one part of the sum and you know the sum.

   Write a word sentence to show the problem.

   _____

   **Step 2:** Draw a picture to show the problem. The part you know has been done for you.

   7 postcards from California      **Draw more postcards until you have 11.**

   ☐ ☐ ☐ ☐ ☐ ☐ ☐

   Write a number sentence.

   _____

   **Answer the question:** _____ postcards are not from California.

2. A carton holds 12 eggs. Andre put 8 eggs into a carton. How many more eggs does he need to fill the carton?

   **Step 1:** Write a word sentence and draw a picture to show the problem.

   _____

   Part you know                    Missing part



   Total number of eggs

   **Step 2:** Write a number sentence.

   _____

   **Answer the question:** Andre needs _____ more eggs.

## PRACTICE
Draw a picture to find the missing part.

1. Anna has 14 books. She has 7 mystery books. The rest are books about science. How many science books does she have?

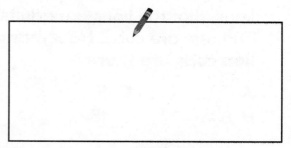

_____

2. Todd has run 9 miles so far this week. He wants to run 15 miles in all this week. How many more miles does he need to run?

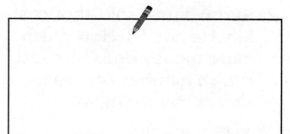

_____

3. Miguel wants to buy a book that costs $15. He has saved $8. How much more money does he need to buy the book?

_____

4. Paul made 3 deliveries this morning. He must make 12 deliveries today. How many more deliveries does he need to make?

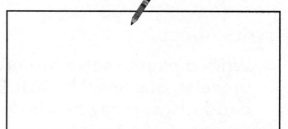

_____

5. Pilar wants to buy a shirt that costs $10. Her sister gives her $4. How much more money does she need?

# TEST-TAKING PRACTICE

Choose the best answer for each problem.

**1.** There are 15 lions in a pride of lions. 8 of the lions are adults. The rest are cubs. **How many lion cubs are there?**

**A** 7      **C** 9
**B** 8      **D** 15

**2.** Kurt wants a shirt that costs $13. He has $8. How much more money does he need? **Which number sentence shows the problem?**

**J** 13 + 8 = 21
**K** 8 + ? = 13
**L** 13 + ? = 8
**M** 8 + 13 = ?

**3.** Jemal has 6 puzzle pieces. There should be 14 puzzle pieces. **How many pieces are missing?**

**A** 5      **C** 7
**B** 6      **D** 8

**4.** Shana has swum 6 laps in the pool. She plans to swim 10 laps. How many more laps will she swim? **Which drawing shows the problem?**

**J**  part you know   missing part

**K**  part you know   missing part

**L**  part you know   missing part

**M**  part you know

## Write About It

**5.** Write a plan to solve this problem: Janelle wants to make a bracelet. She has 9 beads. The finished bracelet will have 16 beads. How many beads does she need?

_____

_____

_____

1. A ☐  B ☐  C ☐  D ☐     3. A ☐  B ☐  C ☐  D ☐
2. J ☐  K ☐  L ☐  M ☐     4. J ☐  K ☐  L ☐  M ☐

● Missing Addends

# Reading a Pictograph

To solve a math problem, you may need to get information from a pictograph.

**A.** Read the title. **What is this pictograph about?**

_cans collected_

**B.** On the left side of the pictograph are the names of people who collected cans.

**How many people collected cans?** _5 people_

Cans Collected

| Sal | 🥫🥫 |
| Cora | 🥫🥫🥫 |
| Pedro | 🥫🥫🥫🥫🥫🥫 |
| Ann | 🥫🥫🥫🥫 |
| Ted | 🥫🥫🥫 |

Key: 🥫 = 1 can

**C.** The key for a pictograph tells what each picture stands for.

What does each 🥫 stand for? _1 can_

**Example 1: How many cans did Pedro collect?**

Read across the row. Count the number of 🥫 next to Pedro's name.

There are ___6___ 🥫 next to his name. So, Pedro

collected ___6___ cans.

**Example 2: Who collected the most cans?**

Find the row that has the most cans. Read across the row to find the name.

___Pedro___ has the most 🥫 next to his name.

So, ___Pedro___ collected the most cans.

## GUIDED PRACTICE

Sometimes each picture in a pictograph stands for more than one item. You can read the key to find how many each picture stands for.

Use the pictograph at the right to answer questions 1 and 2.

1. How many cats does each  stand for?

   _____

Cats in the Cat Show

| Tiger-Striped | 🐱 🐱 🐱 🐱 🐱 |
|---|---|
| Calico | 🐱 🐱 |

**Key:** 🐱 = 2 cats

2. Skip-count by 2 to find how many cats of each kind were in the cat show.

   **Tiger-Striped:** _____

   **Calico:** _____

Use the pictograph at the right to answer questions 3–6.

Magazines Sold

| Hannah | 📖 📖 📖 📖 📖 📖 📖 |
|---|---|
| Malik | 📖 📖 📖 📖 |

**Key:** 📖 = 5 magazines

3. How many magazines does each 📖 stand for?

   _____

4. What number can you skip-count by?

   _____

5. How many magazines did Malik sell?

   _____

6. Skip-count to find the answer.

   How many more magazines did Hannah sell than Malik?

   _____

# PRACTICE

**1.** What is the pictograph about?

_____

_____

**Number of Visitors to the Art Show**

| Monday | 웃웃웃웃웃웃웃웃 |
|---|---|
| Tuesday | 웃웃웃웃 |
| Wednesday | 웃웃웃웃웃웃 |
| Thursday | 웃웃웃 |
| Friday | 웃웃웃웃웃웃웃웃웃웃웃 |

**Key:** 웃 = 5 people

**2.** What does each 웃 stand for?

_____

**3.** How many people visited the art show on Tuesday?

_____

**4.** On which day did the most people visit the art show?

_____

**5.** On which day did 30 people visit the art show?

_____

**6.** How many more people visited the art show on Monday than on Tuesday?

_____

**7.** How many fewer people visited the art show on Wednesday than on Friday?

_____

**8.** Did more people visit the art show on the two days, Wednesday and Thursday, or on Friday?

_____

● **Basic Facts**

# TEST-TAKING PRACTICE

Use the pictograph. Choose the best answer for each problem.

### Votes for Best Clown

| KoKo | |
|------|------|
| Muffy | |
| Bop | |
| Poppy | |

Key: = 10 votes

**1. How many clowns got votes?**

A 4          C 300

B 40         D Not given

**2. How many votes did KoKo get?**

J 6          L 30

K 12         M 60

**3. Which clown got 20 votes?**

A Koko       C Poppy

B Bop        D Muffy

**4. Who got 20 more votes than Bop?**

J Koko       L Poppy

K Bop        M Muffy

**5. Who got fewer than 30 votes?**

A Muffy and Bop

B Koko

C Poppy and Muffy

D Poppy

## Write About It

**6. Write about how you found the answer to problem 4.**

_____

_____

_____

1. A ☐  B ☐  C ☐  D ☐        4. J ☐  K ☐  L ☐  M ☐

2. J ☐  K ☐  L ☐  M ☐        5. A ☐  B ☐  C ☐  D ☐

3. A ☐  B ☐  C ☐  D ☐

© 1999 Metropolitan Teaching & Learning Co.

● Basic Facts

# Making a Diagram

Sometimes it is useful to round numbers up or down to solve a problem. You can make a number-line diagram to help you round.

**Example:** The club can buy a pack of paper with 40 sheets or one with 30 sheets. The newsletter has 38 pages. Which pack should they buy?

**A.** Round 38 to the nearest 10 to decide. The number 38 is between 30 and 40. Draw a number-line mountain for the numbers from 30 to 40. The top of the mountain is the middle number, 35.

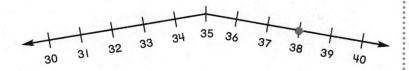

RULES FOR ROUNDING

If the digit in the ones place is 5 or greater, round up to the nearest 10. If the digit in the ones place is less than 5, round down to the nearest 10.

**B.** Make a dot at the mark labeled 38.

**C.** Pretend your dot could roll down the mountain to the nearest ten.

**To which ten would it roll?** _____40_____

**Answer the question:** They should buy

___the pack with 40 pages___ .

## GUIDED PRACTICE

Round the number up or down. Use the
number line to help. Ring one.

1. There are 24 students in John's class. About how
   many students are there?

   about 20 students

   about 30 students

2. Mr. James sold 76 peaches. About how many
   peaches did he sell?

   about 70 peaches

   about 80 peaches

Now try rounding to the nearest hundred.
Use the number line. Look at the digit in the tens place.
Ring the letter of the best answer.

3. The school cafeteria served 570 lunches. About how
   many lunches were served?

   about 500 lunches

   about 600 lunches

4. 120 people came to the play. About how many
   people came to the play?

   about 100 people

   about 200 people

   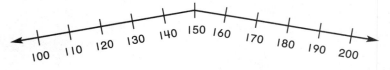

## PRACTICE
Draw a number-line mountain to help you round to
the nearest ten or the nearest hundred.

1. A puppy is 63 days old. About how
   old is the puppy?
   **Round to the nearest ten.**

_____

2. Kiko received 260 votes. About how many votes
   did Kiko receive?
   **Round to the nearest hundred.**

_____

3. A table costs $220. About how much does the
   table cost?
   **Round to the nearest hundred.**

_____

4. A shirt costs $35. About how much does the
   shirt cost?
   **Round to the nearest ten.**

_____

5. The carnival sold 480 tickets. About how many
   tickets were sold?
   **Round to the nearest hundred.**

_____

Choose the best answer for each problem.

**1.** Joan has 346 cards in her sports-card collection. **To the nearest hundred, about how many cards does she have?**

A 300    C 350
B 340    D 400

**2.** Vera read 22 books. **To the nearest ten, about how many books did she read?**

J 10    L 25
K 20    M 30

**3.** James saved $360. **To the nearest hundred, about how much did he save?**

A $300    C $370
B $350    D $400

**4.** There are 55 passengers on the bus. **To the nearest ten, about how many passengers are on the bus?**

J 5    L 60
K 50    M 100

**5.** The bus ticket cost $180. **To the nearest hundred, about how much did it cost?**

A $100    C $300
B $200    D $400

## Write About It

**6.** The newspaper says that about 50 people came to a school board meeting. This number was rounded to the nearest ten. **How many people could have come to the meeting? Explain your thinking.**

_____

_____

1. A ☐   B ☐   C ☐   D ☐     4. J ☐   K ☐   L ☐   M ☐

2. J ☐   K ☐   L ☐   M ☐     5. A ☐   B ☐   C ☐   D ☐

3. A ☐   B ☐   C ☐   D ☐

# Using Mental Math

You can use the addition and subtraction facts you know to solve problems with large numbers.

**Example 1:** It is 90 miles from Milwaukee to Chicago. Fela leaves Milwaukee and stops to eat after 30 miles. How many more miles is it to Chicago?

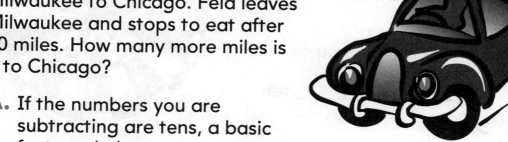

**A.** If the numbers you are subtracting are tens, a basic fact can help.

    *THINK:* **90 – 30 is the same as** __9__ **tens –** __3__ **tens**

**B. Subtract to solve the problem.**

    9 tens – 3 tens = 6 tens    So, __90__ – __30__ = __60__

    **Answer the question:** It is __60 more miles__ to Chicago.

**C.** You can use mental math to solve problems with hundreds, too.

    **Example 2:** The track team walked 300 meters and then ran 500 meters. How many meters in all?

    **Step 1:** Use a basic fact to help you add.

    *THINK:* **300 + 500 is the same as**

        __3__ **hundreds +** __5__ **hundreds**

    **Step 2:** Add.

    3 hundreds + 5 hundreds = 8 hundreds

    So, __300__ + __500__ = __800__

    **Answer the question:** __800__ meters in all.

© 1999 Metropolitan Teaching & Learning Co.

## GUIDED PRACTICE

1. Billy scored 50 points on his first turn at a target game. He scored 40 points on his second turn. What was his total score?

    **Step 1:** Think of a basic fact you can use.

    50 + 40 is the same as

    _____ tens + _____ tens

    **Step 2:** Solve.

    _____ tens + _____ tens = _____ tens

    So, _____ + _____ = _____

    **Answer the question:** Billy's total score was _____ points.

2. A race is 400 meters long. Kathy has run 100 meters. How many more meters does she need to run?

    **Step 1:** Use a basic fact to solve with mental math.

    _____ – _____ is the same as

    _____ hundreds – _____ hundred

    **Step 2:** Solve.

    400 – 100 = _____

    **Answer the question:** She needs to run _____ meters more.

## PRACTICE
Use mental math to add or subtract.

1. A large box holds 500 sheets of paper. A smaller box holds 300 sheets of paper. How many sheets of paper are in the two boxes?

   _____ sheets of paper

2. Students had 600 tickets to sell for the school play. They have sold 400 tickets so far. How many tickets have not been sold?

   _____ tickets

3. Al has 30 souvenir pins in his collection. James has 60 pins in his collection. How many pins do they have together?

   _____ pins

4. Mai bought 50 stamps. Then she used 30 of the stamps. How many stamps does she have left?

   _____ stamps

5. Ms. Wong needs to drive 150 miles to visit a friend. If she has driven 70 miles so far, how much farther must she drive?

   _____ miles

6. The dairy sold 700 half-gallon cartons of milk and 200 gallon cartons of milk. How many cartons did it sell?

   _____ cartons

## TEST-TAKING PRACTICE

Choose the best answer for each problem.

**1.** Mark rode his bike 30 miles in the morning. He rode 10 miles in the afternoon. **How many miles did he ride?**

**Which fact could be used to solve the problem?**

**A** 3 + 1 = 4
**B** 3 – 1 = 2
**C** 3 + 10 = 33
**D** Not given

**2.** Kayla bought two boxes of paper. One box had 500 sheets of paper. The other had 200 sheets. **How many sheets of paper did Kayla buy?**

**J** 70          **L** 500
**K** 200        **M** 700

**3.** An apartment building is 50 feet tall. A lamppost is 30 feet tall. **How much taller is the building than the lamppost?**

**A** 2 feet      **C** 30 feet
**B** 20 feet     **D** 50 feet

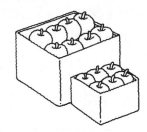

**4.** A small box of fruit weighs 30 pounds. A large box weighs 40 pounds. **How much do the boxes weigh together?**

**J** 7 pounds    **L** 40 pounds
**K** 10 pounds   **M** 70 pounds

## Write About It

**5.** How can you use mental math to find the difference: 800 – 600 = ?

_____

_____

1. A ☐  B ☐  C ☐  D ☐        3. A ☐  B ☐  C ☐  D ☐
2. J ☐  K ☐  L ☐  M ☐        4. J ☐  K ☐  L ☐  M ☐

● Adding and Subtracting Larger Numbers

# Comparing and Ordering Numbers

Deciding whether the answer is a word or a number helps you tell if your answer makes sense.

**Example 1:** Mark had 358 baseball cards. Lori had 394 baseball cards. Which is the greater amount?

**A.** Decide whether the answer will be numbers or words.

**THINK:** The question asks, "<u>Which amount</u> is greater?" An amount is a number. So, your answer will be a **number.**

**B. Compare the numbers to find the answer.**

___394___ > ___358___

**Answer the question:** Which amount is greater?

___394___

**Example 2:** John drove 275 miles this month. Maria drove 302 miles this month. Who drove more miles?

**Step 1:** Decide whether the answer will be numbers or words.

**THINK:** The question asks, "<u>Who</u> drove more miles?" The answer will be a name. A name is a **word.**

**Step 2: Compare the numbers.**

275 _<_ 302

Then answer the question with a word.

**Answer the question:** Who drove more miles? __Maria__

## GUIDED PRACTICE

**I.** On Friday 507 people came to the play. On Saturday 417 people came to the play. On which day did fewer people come to the play?

**Step 1:** Will the answer be a number or a word? Ring one.

        number        word

**Step 2:** Compare the numbers.

_____ is less than _____

**Answer the question:** Fewer people came on

_____.

To solve a problem, sometimes you have to put three or more numbers in order.

**2.** Shawn has 325 stickers and Jerry has 372 stickers. David has 354 stickers. How many stickers does the boy with the most have?

**Step 1:** Will the answer be a number or a word? Ring one.

        number        word

**Step 2:** Place the numbers in order from least to greatest.

_____

**Answer the question:** The boy with the most

stickers has _____.

> Play this Friday and Saturday!

## PRACTICE
Decide whether the answer will be words or numbers.
Solve.

1. On Monday Lourdes rode the bus 208 miles. On Tuesday she rode 179 miles. On which day did she ride more miles?

_____

2. Gene has 54 art books and 58 storybooks. Does he have more art books or more storybooks?

_____

3. Hank Aaron hit 755 home runs, Reggie Jackson hit 563 home runs, and Willie Mays hit 660 home runs. How many home runs were hit by the player who hit the most home runs?

_____

4. Nita saved $107 in 1999. She saved $170 in 2000. In which year did she save more money?

_____

5. A bead kit costs $14 at the Bead Store. The same bead kit costs $16 at the Craft Store. Which price is less?

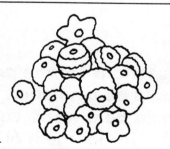

_____

6. Jewell took two trips. She flew 324 miles to Texas and 319 miles to Mexico. On which trip did she fly more miles?

_____

# TEST-TAKING PRACTICE

Choose the best answer for each problem.

**1.** Bill weighed four dogs. Sparky weighed 46 pounds. Dolly weighed 54 pounds. Prince weighed 42 pounds, and Bear weighed 49 pounds. **Which dog weighed the least?**

**A** Sparky  **C** Prince
**B** Dolly   **D** Bear

**2.** There are three colors of jelly beans in the jar. You have to guess which color most of the jelly beans are. **How do you write your answer?**

**J** with numbers
**K** with words
**L** with both numbers and words
**M** Not given

**3.** Jan swam 600 meters on Monday and 550 meters on Tuesday. He swam 775 meters on Wednesday and 750 meters on Thursday. **On which day did he swim the farthest?**

**A** Monday
**B** Tuesday
**C** Wednesday
**D** Thursday

**4.** Matt wrote 78, 89, and 79 on the board. **Which shows the numbers in order from greatest to least?**

**J** 78, 79, 89
**K** 78, 89, 79
**L** 89, 78, 79
**M** 89, 79, 78

## Write About It

**5. Write two questions for the problem below. The answer to one question should be a number. The answer to the other question should be a word.** Luis is 60 inches tall. Jamal is 59 inches tall, and George is 61 inches tall.

_____

_____

_____

1. A ☐  B ☐  C ☐  D ☐     3. A ☐  B ☐  C ☐  D ☐
2. J ☐  K ☐  L ☐  M ☐     4. J ☐  K ☐  L ☐  M ☐

© 1999 Metropolitan Teaching & Learning Co.

32                                    • Comparing Numbers

Name _____

# Test-Taking Skill: Writing a Plan

Some questions on tests ask you to explain how you solve a problem. You can write a plan to show the steps you take to find the answer.

**Example:** Lena read 4 books last week and 6 books the week before. She read 2 books this week. How many books did Lena read in these 3 weeks?

**A.** **Read the problem carefully. Decide what kind of answer you are looking for.**

The answer is the total number of books Lena read in 3 weeks.

**B.** **Write a plan for finding the answer. You can number the steps you will take.**

1. Find out how many books she read each week. I can get that information from the problem.

2. Add the 3 numbers.

3. I'll add 2 numbers first, then add the other number.

**C.** **Solve the problem following the steps of your plan.**

1. 4 books + 6 books + 2 books

2.  4
  + 6
  ____

3.  10
  + 2
  ____

**D.** **Answer the question in the problem:**

Lena read _____ books.

# TEST-TAKING PRACTICE

Write a plan to solve each problem. Follow the steps of your plan.

**1.** Karl makes a paper-clip chain that is 76 inches long. Ann makes one that is 69 inches long, and Gordy makes one that is 74 inches long. Who makes the longest chain?

**Step 1:** Get the information you need from the problem.

**Step 2:** Write a plan.

_____

_____

_____

_____

**Step 3:** Follow your plan to answer the question.

_____

_____

_____

_____

**2.** Yuri makes a hat with ribbons. He uses all of the blue ribbons and green ribbons from the box. How many ribbons does he put on his hat?

| Ribbons in Box | |
|---|---|
| Color | Number |
| red | 8 |
| blue | 7 |
| green | 3 |

**Step 1:** Write a plan.

_____

_____

_____

**Step 2:** Follow your plan to answer the question.

_____

_____

_____

_____

# Using a Calendar

Reading a calendar can help you find information to solve problems about dates and the days of the week.

**A.** The title of a calendar is the name of a month.

| October | | | | | | |
|---|---|---|---|---|---|---|
| Sunday | Monday | Tuesday | Wednesday | Thursday | Friday | Saturday |
| | | 1 | 2 | 3 | 4 | 5 |
| 6 | 7 | 8 | 9 | 10 | 11 | 12 |
| 13 | 14 | 15 | 16 | 17 | 18 | 19 |
| 20 | 21 | 22 | 23 | 24 | 25 | 26 |
| 27 | 28 | 29 | 30 | 31 | | |

**What month is this calendar for?**

_____October_____

**B.** The days of the week are listed in order across the top row. Each row of the calendar shows one week.

**Which day is the first day of the week on this calendar?**

_____Sunday_____

**C.** The days of the month are numbered. The number is the date.

**What day of the week is October 1?**

_____Tuesday_____

**D.** Use the calendar to answer questions.

**Example:** What date is the second Monday in October?

**Step 1:** Find Monday in the top row.

**Step 2:** Find the first box in the Monday column with a date in it. That is the first Monday in the month. Now move down one row to find the date of the next Monday.

**Answer the question:** The second Monday in October is _____October 14_____.

Use the calendar to answer the questions.

## April

| Sunday | Monday | Tuesday | Wednesday | Thursday | Friday | Saturday |
|---|---|---|---|---|---|---|
|  |  |  |  |  | 1 | 2 |
| 3 | 4 | 5 | 6 | 7 | 8 | 9 |
| 10 | 11 | 12 | 13 | 14 | 15 | 16 |
| 17 | 18 | 19 | 20 | 21 | 22 | 23 |
| 24 | 25 | 26 | 27 | 28 | 29 | 30 |

1. What month does the calendar show?

   _____

2. What day of the week is April 5?

   _____

3. What is the date of the third Saturday in April?

   _____

4. Today is April 7. The French Club meets two weeks from today. On what date will the club meet?

   **Step 1:** Find the box for April 7.

   **Step 2:** Count down two boxes from April 7.

   **Answer the question:** The French Club will meet

   _____

5. Karan's birthday was 17 days ago. Today is April 22. On what day of the week was her birthday?

   **Step 1:** Find April 22.

   **Step 2:** Count back 17 days from April 22. Then look at the word at the top of the column to find out the day of the week.

   **Or: THINK:** There are 7 days in a week, so there are 14 days in two weeks.

   Move up 2 rows from April 22 to April 8.

   Count back 3 days to make a total of 17 days.

   **Answer the question:** Karan's birthday was on

   _____.

## PRACTICE

Use the calendar to solve the problems.

| December | | | | | | |
|---|---|---|---|---|---|---|
| Sunday | Monday | Tuesday | Wednesday | Thursday | Friday | Saturday |
| | 1 | 2 | 3 | 4 | 5 | 6 |
| 7 | 8 | 9 | 10 | 11 | 12 | 13 |
| 14 | 15 | 16 | 17 | 18 | 19 | 20 |
| 21 | 22 | 23 | 24 | 25 | 26 | 27 |
| 28 | 29 | 30 | 31 | | | |

1. What is the date of the last Saturday in this month?

   _____

2. The school winter vacation will begin December 23. What day of the week is this?

   _____

3. The school band is giving a concert on December 16. Today is December 2. How many weeks are there until the concert?

   _____

4. Today is December 8. Kent will visit the doctor in 5 days. What date will that be?

   _____

5. Tanya practices for the play every Monday. On which dates in December will she practice?

   _____

   _____

   _____

6. The chorus meets every Thursday. Today is December 16. When did the chorus last meet?

   _____

7. The Games Club meets every Tuesday. How many meetings do they have in December?

   _____

# TEST-TAKING PRACTICE

Choose the best answer for each problem.

## February

| Sunday | Monday | Tuesday | Wednesday | Thursday | Friday | Saturday |
|--------|--------|---------|-----------|----------|--------|----------|
|        | 1      | 2       | 3         | 4        | 5      | 6        |
| 7      | 8      | 9       | 10        | 11       | 12     | 13       |
| 14     | 15     | 16      | 17        | 18       | 19     | 20       |
| 21     | 22     | 23      | 24        | 25       | 26     | 27       |
| 28     |        |         |           |          |        |          |

**1. On what day of the week is the last day in February?**

**A** Sunday    **C** Monday
**B** Wednesday    **D** Saturday

**2.** Jean will visit the dentist on the third Thursday of the month. **On what date will she visit?**

**J** February 4
**K** February 11
**L** February 18
**M** February 25

**3.** Ron has hockey practice every Wednesday. Today is February 14. **What is the date of his next practice?**

**A** February 5
**B** February 15
**C** February 16
**D** February 17

**4.** Today is February 2. Alonzo needs to return a library book in three weeks. **What is the last date he can return the book?**

**J** February 5
**K** February 23
**L** February 30
**M** Not given

## Write About It

**5.** Suppose February 1 was on Wednesday. **On what day of the week would February 28 be? How did you find your answer?**

_____

_____

| | | | |
|---|---|---|---|
| 1. A ☐ B ☐ C ☐ D ☐ | | 3. A ☐ B ☐ C ☐ D ☐ | |
| 2. J ☐ K ☐ L ☐ M ☐ | | 4. J ☐ K ☐ L ☐ M ☐ | |

© 1999 Metropolitan Teaching & Learning Co.

● Calendars

# Reading a Schedule

A schedule is a table of information about when events are supposed to happen.

| School Bus Schedule | |
| --- | --- |
| **Bus Stop** | **Time A.M.** |
| Oak Street | 7:15 |
| Lime Street | 7:23 |
| River Street | 7:35 |
| Bloom Street | 7:41 |
| School | 8:00 |

**A.** The title tells you what the schedule is about.

**What does the title tell you?** Write the missing words.

This is a ___school bus___ schedule.

**B.** Read the first column in the schedule. It lists the streets at which the bus stops. **How many different streets does the bus stop at before it stops at school?**

___4 streets___

**What is the third street at which the bus stops?**

___River Street___

**C.** The second column tells what time the bus should stop at each street. **What time does the bus stop at Oak Street?**

___7:15 A.M.___

**What time does the bus get to school?** ___8:00 A.M.___

## GUIDED PRACTICE

Use the bus schedule to answer the questions.

1. What is the schedule about?

   _____

   _____

| Green County Bus Schedule | |
|---|---|
| Town | Time P.M. |
| Green | 3:04 |
| Milltown | 3:25 |
| Union | 4:08 |
| Anderson | 4:40 |
| Sundale | 5:45 |
| Parker | 6:23 |

2. At what time should the bus be in Milltown?

   _____

3. At what time should the bus be in Sundale?

   _____

4. What town is the last bus stop on the schedule?

   _____

5. The bus is in Union at 4:00 P.M. Is it early or late?

   **Step 1:** Find Union on the schedule.

   What time should the bus be in Union? _____

   **Step 2:** Compare the times.

   Is 4:00 P.M. before or after 4:08 P.M.? _____

   **THINK:** If the bus leaves before the time on the schedule, it is early.

   If the bus leaves after the time on the schedule, it is late.

   **Answer the question:** The bus is _____.

## PRACTICE

Use the train schedule to solve the problems.

| Long County Train Schedule | |
|---|---|
| Town | Time A.M. |
| Long | 7:00 |
| Blue Hill | 7:12 |
| Sand Cove | 7:48 |
| Seaside | 8:20 |
| Glen | 8:47 |
| Grant | 9:15 |

1. What does the schedule show?

_____

_____

2. How many stops does the train make?

_____

3. At what time should the train be in Grant?

_____

4. When should the train be in Sand Cove?

_____

5. The train gets to Blue Hill at 7:15 A.M. Is it early or late?

_____

6. The train has just left Sand Cove. Where does it stop next?

_____

7. What town is the fifth stop on the schedule?

_____

8. Kelly got to the Long train station at 6:57 A.M. Was she early or late for the train?

_____

9. Kelly took the train from Long to Seaside. What stops did she pass before she got off?

_____

10. Matt got on the train at 7:12 A.M. What station did he get on at?

_____

Choose the best answer for each problem.

| Island Ferry Schedule | |
|---|---|
| Island | Time |
| Portland | 10:30 A.M. |
| King Island | 11:20 A.M. |
| Bear Island | 12:15 P.M. |
| Fog Island | 1:55 P.M. |
| Shark Island | 3:05 P.M. |
| Bird Island | 4:25 P.M. |
| Portland | 6:00 P.M. |

**2. What time should the ferry be at Fog Island?**

**J** 10:30 A.M.
**K** 12:15 P.M.
**L** 1:55 P.M.
**M** 3:05 P.M.

**3. What is the ferry stop before Bird Island?**

**A** Fog Island
**B** Portland
**C** Bear Island
**D** Shark Island

**1. What island is the second stop on the schedule?**

**A** Portland
**B** King Island
**C** Fog Island
**D** Bird Island

**4. The ferry docks at Fog Island at 2:05 P.M. Which sentence is true?**

**J** The ferry is early.
**K** The ferry is on time.
**L** The ferry is late.
**M** Not given

## Write About It

**5.** Use the ferry schedule. Jim got on the ferry at King Island. He got off at Bird Island. **How many stops did the ferry make before he reached Bird Island? Explain how you found the answer.**

_____

_____

1. A☐  B☐  C☐  D☐      3. A☐  B☐  C☐  D☐

2. J☐  K☐  L☐  M☐      4. J☐  K☐  L☐  M☐

● Schedules

# Counting Money

You can draw the coins and count their values to solve money problems.

**Example:** Keiko has 3 dimes, I quarter, 2 pennies, and I nickel. How much money does she have?

**A.** Draw the coins. Label each coin with how many cents it is worth.

| 3 dimes | I quarter | 2 pennies | I nickel |
|---------|-----------|-----------|----------|
| ⑩ ⑩ ⑩ | ㉕ | ① ① | ⑤ |

**B.** Count the value of the coins you drew.

Cross out each coin as you count it.

**THINK:** What is the easiest way to count the money?

**C.** For this set of coins, you can start with the quarter.

Count on the nickel.

Count on the dimes.

Count on the pennies.

**Answer the question:** Keiko has _____62¢_____.

● Value of Money

43

## GUIDED PRACTICE

Draw coins to solve the problem.

**1.** Don has 2 nickels, 1 quarter, and 2 dimes. How much money does he have?

**Step 1:** Draw the coins.

**Step 2:** Count the value of the coins. Cross out each coin as you count it.

Try counting different ways. Try this way first.

**Count on the nickels.** (5) (5) (25) (10) (10)

**Count on the dimes.** (5) (5) (25) (10) (10)

**Count on the quarter.** (5) (5) (25) (10) (10)

Now count another way.

**Count the quarter.** (5) (5) (25) (10) (10)

**Count on the dimes.** (5) (5) (25) (10) (10)

**Count on the nickels.** (5) (5) (25) (10) (10)

How much money does he have? _____

**2.** Which way of counting was easier for you, the first or the second?

_____

## PRACTICE
Draw coins to solve the problems.

1. Tia has 2 pennies, 1 quarter, 1 nickel, and 2 dimes. How much money does she have?

   _____

2. Jamal paid for his milk and got change. He got 3 dimes, 1 quarter, and 3 nickels in change. How much was his change worth?

   _____

3. Kenya bought juice. She paid with 2 nickels, 2 quarters, and 3 pennies. How much did she pay?

   _____

4. Leslie counted the value of the coins in her pocket. She had 1 nickel, 3 pennies, 2 dimes, and 2 quarters. What were her coins worth?

   _____

## TEST-TAKING PRACTICE

Choose the best answer for each problem.

1. Betty bought an apple and got some change. She got 1 dime, 4 pennies, and 1 quarter. **How much is her change worth?**

   **A** 18¢    **C** 39¢
   **B** 34¢    **D** 55¢

2. Paul has 2 dimes, 2 pennies, and 1 nickel. **How much money does he have?**

   **J** 20¢    **L** 25¢
   **K** 22¢    **M** 27¢

3. Lori Ann has 2 quarters, 1 nickel, and 1 dime. **How much money does she have?**

   **A** 60¢    **C** 70¢
   **B** 65¢    **D** Not given

4. Steve bought a whistle. He paid for it with 1 quarter, 1 nickel, 2 pennies, and 1 dime. **How much did the whistle cost?**

   **J** 32¢    **L** 42¢
   **K** 41¢    **M** 51¢

5. Jim has 3 dimes. His sister gave him 2 more dimes and 5 pennies. **How much money does he have now?**

   **A** 30¢    **C** 55¢
   **B** 50¢    **D** 80¢

## Write About It

6. Nancy has 3 dimes, 4 pennies, and 2 nickels in her purse. **How much money does she have? Describe how you would solve this problem.**

_____

_____

| | | |
|---|---|---|
| 1. A ☐ B ☐ C ☐ D ☐ | 4. J ☐ K ☐ L ☐ M ☐ | |
| 2. J ☐ K ☐ L ☐ M ☐ | 5. A ☐ B ☐ C ☐ D ☐ | |
| 3. A ☐ B ☐ C ☐ D ☐ | | |

© 1999 Metropolitan Teaching & Learning Co.

● Value of Money

# Reading Bar Graphs

You can use a bar graph to compare data.

**A.** This graph is about how much money Jessica saved each month.

**B.** The label at the bottom of the graph tells that the bars show months. The label below each bar tells you what month that bar shows.

**What does the fourth bar show?** Complete the sentence.

**The bar shows how much Jessica saved in**

_____October_____.

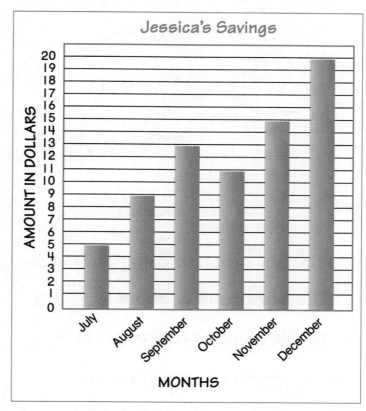

Jessica's Savings

**C.** The label on the left side of the graph says: **Amount in Dollars.** It tells you what the numbers on the left side of the graph stand for.

**What does 11 stand for?** _____11 dollars_____

**D. How much money did Jessica save in July?**

**Step 1:** Find the bar for July.

**Step 2:** Read across to the left to the number.

The number tells you how many dollars Jessica saved in July.

**Answer the question:** Jessica saved

_____5 dollars_____ in July.

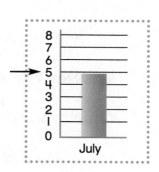

© 1999 Metropolitan Teaching & Learning Co.

## GUIDED PRACTICE

In this bar graph, the bars go from left to right.

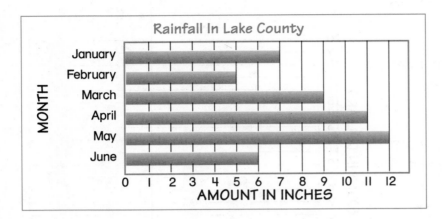

Use the bar graph to complete the sentences.

**1. The bar graph is about** _____.

**2. The amount of rain is given in** _____.

Use the graph to answer the questions.

**3. How much rain did Lake County have in April?** _____

**4. In which month did Lake County have 6 inches of rain?**

_____

5. Use the bars to compare information. Which month had the least rain?

   **Step 1:** Find the shortest bar.

   **Step 2:** Read the label that tells the month.

   **Answer the question:** _____ had the least rain.

6. Which month had more rain than April?

   **Step 1:** Find the bar for April.

   **Step 2:** Find a bar that is longer. Read the label.

   **Answer the question:** _____ had more rain than April.

Name _____

## PRACTICE
Use the bar graph to solve the problems.

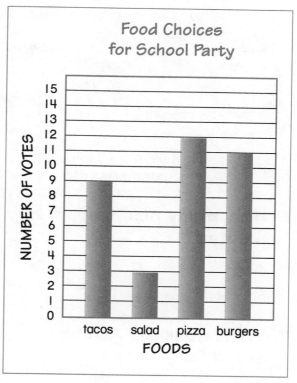

**Food Choices for School Party**

1. What is the bar graph about?

   _____

   _____

2. What do the numbers at the left stand for?

   _____

3. How many kinds of food are shown on the graph?

   _____

4. How many votes were counted for tacos?

   _____

5. Which food got only 3 votes?

   _____

6. How many votes were counted for burgers?

   _____

7. Which food got 12 votes?

   _____

8. Compare the lengths of the bars. Which of these foods got the most votes?

   _____

9. Which of these foods got more votes than tacos?

   _____

● Comparing Data

# TEST-TAKING PRACTICE

Choose the best answer for each problem.

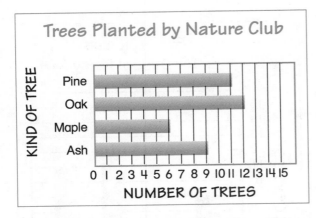

**Trees Planted by Nature Club**

KIND OF TREE: Pine, Oak, Maple, Ash

NUMBER OF TREES: 0 1 2 3 4 5 6 7 8 9 10 11 12 13 14 15

**1. How many pine trees were planted?**

A 6          C 11

B 9          D 14

**2. What does the Ash bar stand for?**

J 9 trees

K 9 pines

L 11 houses

M Not given

**3. Which kind of tree was planted least?**

A Pine          C Maple

B Oak           D Ash

**4. Which kind of tree was planted most?**

J Pine          L Maple

K Oak           M Ash

**5. Which kind of tree was planted less often than ash trees?**

A Pine          C Maple

B Oak           D Ash

## Write About It

**6. Write how you would find how many more oak trees were planted than maple trees. Then find the answer.**

_____

_____

1. A ☐  B ☐  C ☐  D ☐          4. J ☐  K ☐  L ☐  M ☐

2. J ☐  K ☐  L ☐  M ☐          5. A ☐  B ☐  C ☐  D ☐

3. A ☐  B ☐  C ☐  D ☐

● Comparing Data

# Using a Bar Graph

To solve a math problem, you may need to find information on a bar graph.

**A.** **What is the graph about?** Ring one.

- (how many buttons were sold)

- how many colors of buttons

**B.** Each bar shows one color of button.

**How many colors of buttons were sold?**

_____4 colors_____

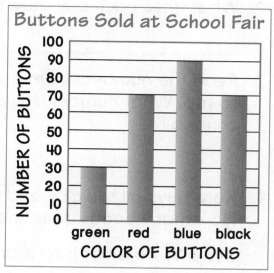

Buttons Sold at School Fair

**C.** Each line on the graph is labeled with a number.
**What number do you count by?** _____10_____

**Which color button sold best?** _____blue_____

**D.** **You can use the bar graph to solve a problem.**

**Example:** How many black buttons and green buttons were sold?

**Step 1:** Find the bars for black buttons and green buttons.

**How many black buttons were sold?** _____70_____

**How many green buttons were sold?** _____30_____

**Step 2:** Write a word sentence. Then write a number sentence.

Black buttons   +   Green buttons   =   Total buttons

_____70_____   +   _____30_____   =   _____100_____

**Answer the question:** _____100_____ black and green buttons were sold.

# GUIDED PRACTICE

1. What is the graph about?

   _____

2. What does each bar show?

   _____

3. Read the numbers from bottom to top. What number do you count by?

   _____

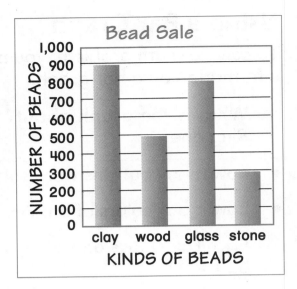

4. Kate buys all the clay and stone beads. How many beads does she buy?

   **Step 1:** Find out how many clay and stone beads there are.

   There are _____ clay beads and _____ stone beads.

   **Step 2:** Write a word sentence.

   _____ beads + _____ beads = _____

   **Answer the question:** How many beads does Kate buy? _____

5. Jim buys all the glass and wood beads. How many beads does he buy?

   **Step 1:** Use the graph to find out how many beads.

   There are _____ glass beads and _____ wood beads.

   **Step 2:** Write a word sentence. Then write a number sentence.

   _____

   _____

   **Answer the question:** Jim buys _____.

## PRACTICE

The bar graph shows how many foreign coins are in the collection.

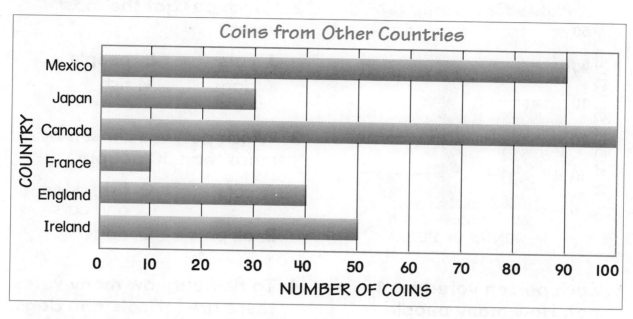

Use the bar graph to answer the questions.

1. How many countries do the coins come from? _____

2. How many coins does each section of the graph show? _____

3. How many coins come from Canada? _____

4. From which country are there 40 coins? _____

5. From which countries are there more than 60 coins?

   _____

6. How many coins are there from England and France together?

   _____

7. How many coins are there in the whole collection?

   _____

## TEST-TAKING PRACTICE

Choose the best answer for each problem.

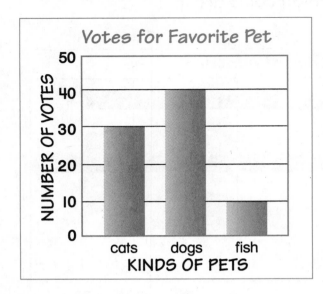

Votes for Favorite Pet

**1.** Each person voted for 1 pet. How many people voted for cats as their favorite pet?

  **A** cats     **C** 30 people

  **B** 3 people   **D** 10 per block

**2.** Which pet got the most votes?

  **J** cats     **L** people

  **K** dogs     **M** fish

**3.** Which pet was chosen by more than 30 people?

  **A** cats     **C** fish, dogs and cats

  **B** all pets   **D** dogs

**4.** To find out how many votes there are for cats and dogs, you would:

  **J** count all the cats and dogs

  **K** add total votes for cats and dogs

  **L** multiply total dogs by 2

  **M** add all of the votes

## Write About It

**5.** How would you find out how many people voted in all?

_____

_____

1. A ☐   B ☐   C ☐   D ☐     3. A ☐   B ☐   C ☐   D ☐

2. J ☐   K ☐   L ☐   M ☐     4. J ☐   K ☐   L ☐   M ☐

● Mental Math with Sums of 10 and 100

# Identifying Important Information

To solve a problem, use only the information you need.

**Example 1:** Mark has 29 shells in his pail. Clara has 37 shells, and Sam has 45 shells. How many shells do Sam and Mark have?

**A.** First, read the problem.

**What are you being asked to find?** Ring one.

- how many shells are in the pail
- (how many shells Sam and Mark have together)

**Do you need to know how many shells**

**Clara has?** _____no_____

**B.** Underline the information you need.

Mark has 29 shells in his pail. Clara has 37 shells, and Sam has 45 shells. How many shells do Sam and Mark have?

**C.** Write a word sentence.

_Sam's shells + Mark's shells =_
_Shells they have together_

Then, write and solve a number sentence.

_45 + 29 = 74_

**Answer the question:** Sam and Mark have _____74 shells_____.

## GUIDED PRACTICE

Use the information on the sign to solve the problems.

1. Jed had $1.00. He bought a hot dog. Sally bought a sandwich. They each bought an orange. How much did Jed spend?

hot dog $0.55

pizza slice $0.60

sandwich $0.75

**Step 1:** Ring the question. Underline the information you need.

apple $0.30

banana $0.25

orange $0.40

**Step 2:** Write a word sentence and a number sentence.

_____ + _____ = _____

_____ + _____ = _____

**Answer the question:** Jed spent _____

2. Ken bought 2 apples and a banana. He gave $0.25 to Meg. Then Meg bought a sandwich and an apple. How much did Meg spend?

**Step 1:** Ring the question. Underline the information you need.

**Step 2:** Write a word sentence and a number sentence.

_____ + _____ = _____

_____ + _____ = _____

**Answer the question:** Meg spent _____.

## PRACTICE
Ring the question. Underline the information you need.

**1.** A marker costs 67¢. A pen costs 32¢. A pencil costs 24¢. How much do a marker and a pencil cost together?

_____

**2.** A red box is 32 inches tall. A green box is 26 inches tall. A blue box is 18 inches tall. Ida puts the blue box on top of the red box. How tall is the stack?

_____

**3.** Joan found 16 shells in the water and 24 shells on the sand. Helga found 27 shells in the water and 31 shells on the sand. How many shells did the two girls find in the water?

_____

**4.** On the first bus there are 23 students and 15 parents. On the second bus there are 18 students and 19 parents. How many students are on the two buses?

_____

**5.** Sue and Brian counted cars that passed. Sue counted 42 black cars. Brian counted 17 blue cars. Then Brian counted 36 red cars and Sue counted 22 white cars. How many cars did Brian count?

_____

● Adding 2-Digit Numbers

# TEST-TAKING PRACTICE

Choose the best answer for each problem.

**1.** Last summer, Lou spent 8 hours painting the porch. He spent 21 hours building a tree house and 12 hours painting it. He also spent 18 hours mowing the lawn. **How many hours did Lou spend painting?**

**A** 18　　　　**C** 28
**B** 20　　　　**D** 39

**2.** There were 16 children and 25 adults on the first train around the park. On the second train, there were 29 children and 17 adults. **How many adults were on the two trains?**

**J** 41　　　　**L** 45
**K** 42　　　　**M** 54

**3.** Skating lessons cost $16 per hour. Swimming lessons cost $25 for a one-and-a-half-hour class. Zoe took 3 skating lessons. Jason took 2 swimming lessons. **How much did Jason pay for his lessons?**

**A** $25　　　　**C** $48
**B** $32　　　　**D** Not given

**4.** At the fair, 4-H club members showed 38 pigs, 21 sheep, 55 chickens, and 24 ducks. **How many four-legged animals did they show?**

**J** 59　　　　**L** 93
**K** 79　　　　**M** 138

## Write About It

**5. Explain the steps you would follow to solve this problem:** A pair of red shoes costs $72. They are on sale for $65. A pair of black shoes cost $69. Mrs. Jimenez bought 2 pairs of red shoes at the sale price. **How much did she spend?**

_____

_____

_____

1. A ☐　B ☐　C ☐　D ☐　　3. A ☐　B ☐　C ☐　D ☐
2. J ☐　K ☐　L ☐　M ☐　　4. J ☐　K ☐　L ☐　M ☐

© 1999 Metropolitan Teaching & Learning Co.

● Adding 2-Digit Numbers

# Using a Map

A map is one way to show information. This map shows how far it is between the homes of people in the walking club.

**A.** Each 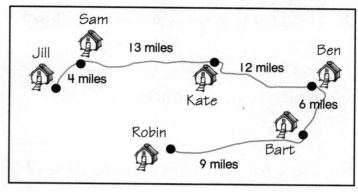 on the map shows the home of the people in the walking club. The ⌣ shows the paths between the homes. The distance between homes is written next to each path.

**How far is it from Robin's home to Bart's home?** ___9 miles___

**B.** Use the map to find out how far it is from one home to the others.

**Example:** How far is it from Ben's home to Jill's home?

**Step 1:** Start at Ben's home.
Follow the path to Jill's home.

**Whose homes would you pass?** ___Kate's and Sam's___

Write a word sentence to show the route.

**Step 2:** Use the map to find the distances. Write the numbers under the words. Then, solve.

Ben's to Kate's + Kate's to Sam's + Sam's to Jill's = Ben's to Jill's

___12___  +  ___13___  +  ___4___  =  ___29___

**Answer the question:** It is ___29 miles___ from Ben's home to Jill's.

## GUIDED PRACTICE

1. How many towns are shown on the map?

   _____

2. How far is it from Ames to Baker?

   _____

3. Which town is nearest to Cady?

   _____

4. How far is it from Glen to Ames?

   **Step 1:** Write a word sentence to show the route.

   _____ to _____ + _____ to _____

   + _____ to _____ = _____ to _____

   **Step 2:** Write and solve a number sentence.

   _____

   **Answer the question:** It is _____ from Glen to Ames.

5. How far is it from Ford to Ebon?

   **Step 1:** Write a word sentence to show the route.

   _____ to _____ + _____ to _____

   + _____ to _____ = _____ to _____

   **Step 2:** Write and solve a number sentence.

   _____

   **Answer the question:** It is _____ from Ford to Ebon.

## PRACTICE

Use the map to answer the questions.

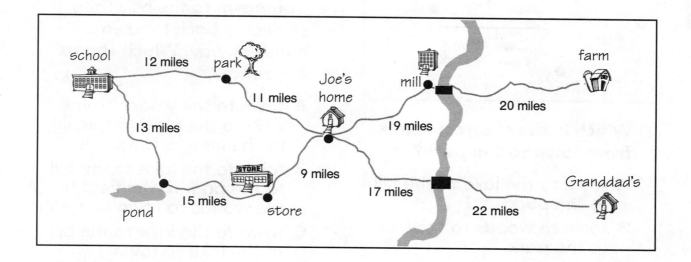

1. Joe rode the bus from home to the school. The bus passed the store and the pond. How far did he go?

   Joe rode _____.

2. Joe went from school to Granddad's. He passed the park. How far did Joe go?

   Joe went _____.

3. From Granddad's, Joe went to the farm. How far did he go?

   Joe went _____.

4. Joe went from the farm to his home. Then he went back to the farm again. How far did Joe go?

   Joe went _____.

5. Sarah went from Joe's home to the mill. Then she went to Granddad's. How far did Sarah go?

   Sarah went _____.

6. Joe and Sarah took different paths to Joe's home from school. Joe went farther. Did Joe go past the pond or past the park?

   Joe went _____.

7. How far did Joe go?

   He went _____.

8. How far did Sarah go?

   Sarah went _____.

● Adding 3 or More Addends

# TEST-TAKING PRACTICE

Choose the best answer for each question.

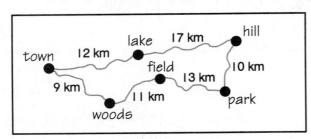

**I. Which is the shortest route from town to the park?**

**A** town to the lake to the hill to the park

**B** town to woods to the field to the park

**C** lake to town to hill to park

**D** Not given

**2.** Suppose you went from the hill to the woods and passed town. **Which number sentence would you use to find the distance?**

**J** 17 + 12 + 9 = 38

**K** 10 + 13 + 11 = 34

**L** 7 + 12 = 29

**M** 12 + 17 + 10 = 39

**3.** Kim took the shorter route from town to the hill. Then she came back to town a different way. **Which shows her route?**

**A** town to the woods to the field to the park to the hill to the lake to town

**B** town to the lake to the hill to the park to the field to the woods to town

**C** town to the lake to the hill to the lake to town

**D** town to the lake to the hill to the field to the woods to town

**4. How far did Kim travel in all?**

**J** 58 km

**K** 62 km

**L** 72 km

**M** 69 km

## Write About It

**5.** Kim wants to know if it is farther from town to the field or from the woods to the park. **How can she find out?**

_____

_____

1. A ☐  B ☐  C ☐  D ☐     3. A ☐  B ☐  C ☐  D ☐

2. J ☐  K ☐  L ☐  M ☐     4. J ☐  K ☐  L ☐  M ☐

© 1999 Metropolitan Teaching & Learning Co.

● Adding 3 or More Addends

# Test-Taking Skill: Focusing on the Question

On a multiple-choice test, it helps to make sure you know what the question is and what kind of answer you are looking for.

**Example:** There were 23 children and 12 adults on the first bus. Another 34 children and 15 adults were on the second bus. How many children were on both buses?

**A** 27 adults

**C** 57 children

**B** 35 children

**D** 84 people

**A. Read the question at the end of the problem. Decide what kind of answer you want.**

How many children were on both buses?

***THINK:*** The answer to questions that ask <u>How many</u> is a **number**.

**B. Decide what operation you will have to do to find the answer.**

The question asks how many children were on <u>both</u> buses, so you will **add** to find the answer.

**C. Decide what answer you are looking for.**

The answer is the total number of children who rode both buses.

**D. Write a number sentence to find the answer.**

23 + 34 = 57

**E. Look for your answer in the list of choices.**

Mark the square labeled C on the answer form.

# TEST-TAKING PRACTICE

Read the question and decide what kind of answer you need. Then choose the right answer from the answer choices.

**I.** Jian worked for 17 days on the project in May. In June, he worked for 23 days. Did he work more days in May or in June?

**A** May　　　　**C** 40 days

**B** 6 days　　　**D** June

**Step 1:** Read the question. Decide what kind of answer you need. Check one.

___ words　　___ numbers.

**Step 2:** Decide what operation you will do to find the answer.

___ add　　___ subtract　　___ compare

**Step 3:** Solve. Choose the correct letter and fill in the box below.

**2.** Linda rode her bike from the school to the library. She passed the grocery store. How many blocks did she ride?

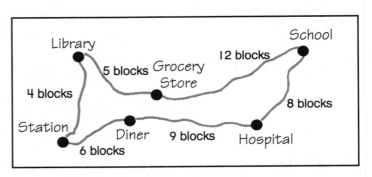

**J** 5　　　　**L** 17

**K** 12　　　**M** 27

**Step 1:** Read the question. Decide what kind of answer you need.

**Step 2:** Decide what operation you will do to find the answer. Solve. Choose the correct letter and fill in the box below.

1. A ☐　B ☐　C ☐　D ☐　　2. J ☐　K ☐　L ☐　M ☐

# Using a Pictograph

To solve problems you may have
to find information on a pictograph.

**A.** Look at the title. Ring the words
to complete the sentence.

**The pictograph shows how many
people came to the carnival:**

• this year    • (each day)

**B.** The labels on the left side of this
pictograph name days of the week.

People at the Carnival

| Thursday | ☺ ☺ |
| Friday | ☺ ☺ |
| Saturday | ☺ ☺ ☺ ☺ |
| Sunday | ☺ ☺ ☺ ☺ ☺ |

Key: ☺ = 10 people

**On what days was the carnival held? Underline the days.**

Monday   Tuesday   Wednesday   <u>Thursday</u>   <u>Friday</u>   <u>Saturday</u>   <u>Sunday</u>

**C.** The key tells you what each ☺ stands for. You can
skip-count by the number shown in the key.

**1 ☺ stands for** _____10 people_____.

**Example:** How many more people came on
Sunday than on Saturday?

**Step 1:** Read the pictograph.

**How many ☺ on Saturday?**

_____4_____ ☺

Skip count to find how
many people.

10, 20, 30, 40

**How many people on**

**Saturday?** _40 people_

**How many ☺ on Sunday?**

_____5_____ ☺

Skip-count to find how
many people.

10, 20, 30, 40, 50

**How many people on**

**Sunday?** _50 people_

**Step 2:** Write a subtraction sentence. _50 — 40 = 10_

**Answer the question:** _10 more people_

© 1999 Metropolitan Teaching & Learning Co.

# GUIDED PRACTICE

1. How many kinds of books are shown on the pictograph?

_____

2. How many books does 1 📕 stand for?

_____

4. By what number can you skip-count?

_____

5. How many more adventure books were borrowed than poetry books?

| Library Books Borrowed in November | |
|---|---|
| Adventure | 📕 📕 📕 |
| Mystery | 📕 📕 📕 📕 |
| History | 📕 📕 |
| Poetry | 📕 |
| Science | 📕 📕 📕 📕 |

Key: 📕 = 100 books

**Step 1:** Read the pictograph. Skip-count to find how many of each kind of book were borrowed.

_____ **adventure books**

_____ **poetry books**

**Step 2:** Write a subtraction sentence.

_____

**Answer the question:** _____ adventure books

6. How many history and science books were borrowed?

**Step 1:** Read the pictograph. Skip-count.

_____ **history books**

_____ **science books**

**Step 2:** Write an addition sentence.

_____

**Answer the question:** _____ books

66

© 1999 Metropolitan Teaching & Learning Co.

## PRACTICE

**1.** Altogether, how many oak trees and ash trees are there?

_____

**2.** How many more maple trees than pine trees are there?

_____

**3.** Are there more pine, ash, and oak trees together than maple trees?

_____

**4.** In all, how many trees are in the neighborhood?

_____

**5.** How many balloons were sold during June and July?

_____

**6.** How many more balloons were sold in August than in June?

_____

**7.** The same number of balloons were sold in September as in May. How many balloons were sold in September?

_____

### Neighborhood Trees

| Maple | 🌳 🌳 🌳 🌳 |
|-------|-----------|
| Oak   | 🌳 🌳 |
| Ash   | 🌳 |
| Pine  | 🌳 🌳 🌳 |

**Key:** 🌳 = 20 trees

### Balloons Sold at the Park

| May    | 🎈 |
|--------|-----|
| June   | 🎈 🎈 |
| July   | 🎈 🎈 🎈 🎈 |
| August | 🎈 🎈 🎈 |

**Key:** 🎈 = 100 balloons

● Subtracting Tens and Hundreds

## TEST-TAKING PRACTICE

Choose the best answer for each problem.

**1.** A pictograph key shows
1 🚗 = 100 cars. **How many cars do 6 🚗 stand for?**

**A** 6　　　　**C** 600

**B** 60　　　　**D** Not given

**2.** A pictograph shows that the same number of people rode bikes to school on Thursday as on Friday. The key shows 1 🚲 = 10 people. **Which sentence about the graph is true?**

**J** There are the same number of 🚲 for Thursday and Friday.

**K** There are more 🚲 for Thursday than for Friday.

**L** There are fewer 🚲 for Thursday than for Friday.

**M** There are more 🚲 for Monday than for Friday.

Use the pictograph.

Gift Magnets Made

| Ed | 🌷🌷 | 🌷🌷 | 🌷🌷 |
| Alison | 🌷🌷 | 🌷🌷 | |
| Gia | 🌷🌷 | | |
| Louise | 🌷🌷 | 🌷🌷 | 🌷🌷 |

Key 🌷🌷 20 magnets

**3. How many magnets did Alison make?**

**A** 2　　　　**C** 40

**B** 20　　　　**D** 200

**4. Together, how many magnets did Gia and Ed make?**

**J** 20　　　　**L** 80

**K** 60　　　　**M** 120

## Write About It

**5. How would you find how many magnets were made by all four people?**

_____

1. A ☐　B ☐　C ☐　D ☐　　3. A ☐　B ☐　C ☐　D ☐

2. J ☐　K ☐　L ☐　M ☐　　4. J ☐　K ☐　L ☐　M ☐

● Subtracting Tens and Hundreds

# Using a Table

To solve some problems, you may need to use a table.

**Example 1:** How much faster is a rabbit than a giraffe?

**A.** Find **rabbit** and **giraffe** in the first column. Read across to the column that shows their speeds.

| Animal Facts | | |
|---|---|---|
| Animal | Top Speed in Miles per Hour | Average Lifespan in Years |
| Cat | 30 | 12 |
| Elk | 45 | 15 |
| Giraffe | 32 | 10 |
| Lion | 50 | 15 |
| Rabbit | 35 | 5 |
| Zebra | 40 | 15 |

**How fast can a rabbit run?**

35 miles per hour

**How fast can a giraffe run?**

32 miles per hour

**B.** Subtract to find the answer. Write a number sentence.

35 − 32 = 3

**Answer the question:** _____ 3 miles per hour _____

**Example 2:** How much longer does the lion live than the cat?

**Step 1:** Find the information on the table.

**A lion lives __15__ years and a cat lives __12__ years.**

**Step 2:** Write the subtraction sentence.

15 − 12 = 3

**Answer the question:** _____ 3 years _____

## GUIDED PRACTICE

**1.** Which book did Joe borrow?

_____

**2.** Which book was borrowed by more than one person?

_____

**3.** Which book was returned on May 21?

_____

**4.** Who borrowed a book on May 13?

_____

| Pet Books Borrowed | | | |
|---|---|---|---|
| Name | Book | Borrowed | Returned |
| Sam | Ponies | May 12 | May 17 |
| Donna | Cats | May 12 | May 15 |
| Joe | Dogs | May 13 | May 17 |
| Mavi | Fish | May 15 | May 21 |
| Ben | Cats | May 17 | May 25 |

**5.** Who borrowed a book for a longer time, Mavi or Sam?

**Step 1:** Find the names Mavi and Sam in the table. Read across to the third and fourth columns. They tell you when books were borrowed and returned.

**Step 2:** Find how many days each book was borrowed.

Subtract the date each book was borrowed from the date it was returned.

Mavi:

_____ – _____ = _____

Mavi borrowed a book

for _____ days.

Sam:

_____ – _____ = _____

Sam borrowed a book

for _____ days.

**Step 3:** Compare to find the answer. _____ > _____

**Answer the question:** _____

Name _____

## PRACTICE
Use the table to answer the questions.

1. How many marbles of each color did Mike have left? Write your answers in the fourth column of the table.

| Mike's Marble Sale | | | |
|---|---|---|---|
| Color | Number at Start | Number Sold | Number Left Over |
| Red | 56 | 23 | |
| Yellow | 34 | 13 | |
| Green | 40 | 38 | |
| Blue | 65 | 49 | |
| Black | 30 | 17 | |
| Pink | 14 | 14 | |

2. To start with, what color marble did Mike have the most of?

_____

3. What color marble did Mike sell the fewest of?

_____

Write a number sentence to find the answer.

4. How many more red marbles than yellow marbles did Mike sell?

_____    _____ more red

5. To start with, how many more blue marbles than green marbles did Mike have?

_____    _____ more blue

6. To start with, how many fewer black marbles than red marbles did Mike have?

_____    _____ fewer black

7. How many more yellow marbles than black marbles did Mike have left over?

_____    _____ more yellow

8. How many fewer pink marbles than green marbles did Mike sell?

_____    _____ fewer pink

● Subtracting 2-Digit Numbers

Choose the best answer for each problem.

| Day | Tickets Sold |
|---|---|
| Friday | 37 |
| Saturday | 48 |
| Sunday | 43 |

**1.** The table shows how many people bought tickets for a play over the weekend. **Which would be the best title for the table?**

**A** Favorite Plays
**B** Play Tickets Sold
**C** This Month at the Theater
**D** Days of the Weekend

**2. To find out how many more people saw the play on Saturday than on Sunday you would:**

**J** add
**K** subtract
**L** compare
**M** Not given

**3.** Some people bought tickets to see the play on Monday. **How would you add that information to the table?**

**A** Add the number of tickets sold to Sunday's tickets
**B** Subtract the number of tickets sold from Sunday's tickets
**C** Make another row below Sunday
**D** Make another column beside Tickets Sold

**4. How many more people saw the play on Sunday than on Friday?**

**J** 3
**K** 6
**L** 37
**M** 43

## Write About It

**5. Write a plan for how you would find out how many fewer tickets were sold on Friday than Saturday.**

_____

_____

1. A ☐ B ☐ C ☐ D ☐    3. A ☐ B ☐ C ☐ D ☐
2. J ☐ K ☐ L ☐ M ☐    4. J ☐ K ☐ L ☐ M ☐

● Subtracting 2-Digit Numbers

# Solving 2-Step Problems

Sometimes you have to do more than one operation to solve a problem.

**Example:** Ling has $5.00. She buys an apple for $0.75 and she buys a sandwich for $3.50. How much change will Ling get?

**A.** First, think about what you need to know to find the answer.

**Do you know how much money Ling has?**

___yes___

**Do you know how much money Ling spends in all?**

___no___

**B.** Ling buys two things. Add to find the total cost.

Write a word sentence and a number sentence.

Cost of apple + Cost of sandwich = Total cost

___$0.75___ + ___$3.50___ = ___$4.25___

**C.** Now you know how much Ling spends. Subtract to find how much change she should get. Write a word sentence and a number sentence.

Money Ling had − Total cost = Change

___$5.00___ − ___$4.25___ = ___$0.75___

**Answer the question:** Ling will get ___$0.75___ in change.

## GUIDED PRACTICE

Decide what to do first. You may use play money to act out each problem.

1. At the toy store, Jenna bought a boat for $3.50 and a Teddy bear for $2.50. She gave the clerk $10.00. How much change did Jenna get?

   **THINK:** Do you know how much

   Jenna gave the clerk? _____

   Do you know how much Jenna spent in all? _____

   **Step 1:** Find out how much Jenna spent in all.

   | Boat | + | Bear | = | Total spent |
   |------|---|------|---|-------------|
   | _____ | + | _____ | = | _____ |

   **Step 2:** Subtract to find out how much change Jenna got.

   | Amount given | – | Total spent | = | Change |
   |--------------|---|-------------|---|--------|
   | _____ | – | _____ | = | _____ |

   **Answer the question:** _____

2. Eric has $6.75 and Tina has $1.50. They want to buy a board game that costs $8.00. How much money will they have left?

   **Step 1: THINK:** What do you know? What do you need to know?

   Write a number sentence to show how much money they have together.

   _____ + _____ = _____

   **Step 2:** Write a number sentence to show how much money they will have after they buy the game.

   _____ – _____ = _____

   **Answer the question:** _____

# PRACTICE
Read each problem carefully. Think about what you need to know. Then solve.

**1.** Max spent $3.50 to buy eggs and $2.25 to buy margarine. His mother gave him $8.00. How much money does Max have left?

_____

**2.** Grover has $7.75. He buys 2 apple tarts that each cost $1.50. How much money does Grover have left?

_____

**3.** Andrea wants to buy a pineapple for $4.25 and a mango for $2.75. She has $6.00. Does she have enough to buy both?

_____

**4.** Eddie buys a slice of pizza for $1.50 and a soda for $1.25. He started with $4.75. How much money does he have left?

_____

**5.** Fay has $4.50. She spends $2.25 to buy yogurt. Now she wants to buy a bag of apples that costs $3.75. How much more money does she need?

_____

**6.** Pablo spent $3.50 on a sandwich and $2.50 on juice. He had $7.50 to start with. How much money does he have left?

_____

# TEST-TAKING PRACTICE

Choose the best answer for each problem.

**1.** Kay had $8.75. She buys a scarf for $3.25 and a hat for $5.50. How much does Kay have now? **Which sentence shows the first step?**

A $0.255
B 8.75 − 3.25
C 8.75 + 3.20
D 3.25 + 5.50

**2.** Abdul spent $2.75 on a patch and $4.50 on a wallet. He had $9.75 to start with. **How much did he have left?**

J $5.25      L $17.00
K $2.50      M $7.25

**3.** Hal buys a cap for $3.50 and a pair of socks for $3.25. He gives the store clerk $7.00. **How much change will Hal get?**

A $0.25      C $6.75
B $3.50      D Not given

**4.** A plain T-shirt costs $7.25. A T-shirt with a picture on it costs $5.00 more than a plain one. Joel has $9.00. **How much more money does he need to buy a T-shirt with a picture on it?**

J $1.75      L $3.25
K $2.25      M $12.25

## Write About It

**5. Describe the steps you would follow to solve this problem:**

Lee has $9.50. He buys his sister a puppet for $4.75 and his brother a puppet for $3.25. He wants to buy a puppet that costs $4.00 for himself. **How much more money does he need?**

_____

_____

_____

_____

1. A ☐  B ☐  C ☐  D ☐      3. A ☐  B ☐  C ☐  D ☐
2. J ☐  K ☐  L ☐  M ☐      4. J ☐  K ☐  L ☐  M ☐

© 1999 Metropolitan Teaching & Learning Co.

● Subtracting Money

# Making a Diagram

To solve some problems you can make a diagram to show the amounts.

**Example:** There are 729 children at camp. 383 of the children are girls. How many are boys?

**A.** Make a diagram to show the amounts. The total number is the whole.

**Do you know the whole?** ___Yes___

Label the whole.

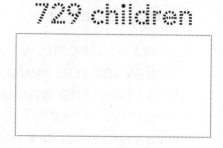

729 children

**B.** The number of girls is one part of the whole.

**How many of the children are girls?**

___383___ are girls. Label one part.

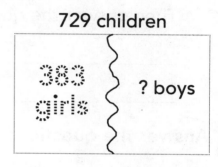

729 children

383 girls    ? boys

**C.** Subtract to find the missing part. Write a word sentence and a number sentence.

Total number — Number of girls = Number of boys

729     —     383     =     346

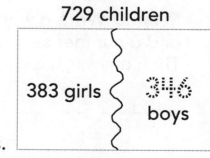

729 children

383 girls    346 boys

**Answer the question:** ___346___ are boys.

## GUIDED PRACTICE

Make a diagram for each problem.

1. One Saturday, 316 people came to the zoo. The next day, Sunday, 275 people came to the zoo. How many people came to the zoo that weekend?

   **Step 1:** Decide what you know and what you need to find. Do you know the whole? Do you know both parts? Draw a diagram to show the problem.

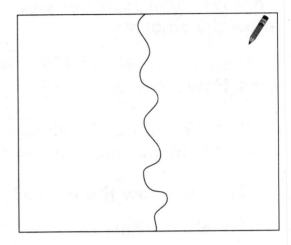

   **Step 2:** Write a word sentence and a number sentence to solve. Then answer the question.

   _____

   _____

**Answer the question:** _____ people

2. The zoomobile has 256 seats. On the last trip there were 117 empty seats. How many people rode the zoomobile on that trip?

   **Step 1:** Draw a diagram to show the problem.

   **Step 2:** Write a word sentence and a number sentence to solve. Then answer the question.

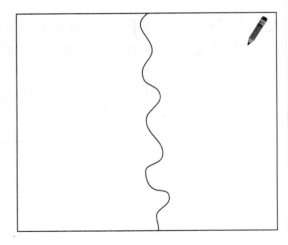

   _____

   _____

**Answer the question:** _____ people

## PRACTICE
Draw a diagram to show the problem.

1. At the Street Fair this year, Gabo the Clown used 673 balloons to make flowers and dogs. She used 392 balloons to make flowers. How many balloons did she use to make dogs?

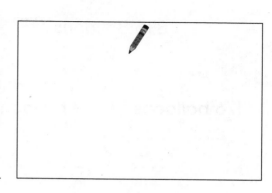

_____

2. The Street Fair committee invited 234 restaurants to have booths. There were 176 restaurants that had booths at the fair. How many did not have booths at the fair?

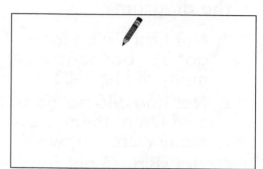

_____

3. The community center sold raffle tickets for $1 apiece. It sold 372 tickets on Saturday and 459 tickets on Sunday. How many dollars worth of tickets did they sell that weekend?

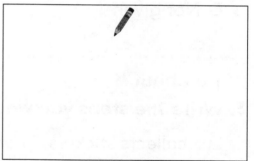

_____

4. Jake's T-Shirts printed 900 shirts to sell at the Street Fair. At the end of the fair, 320 shirts were left over. How many shirts were sold?

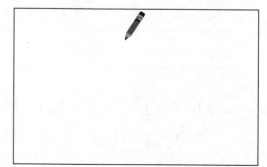

_____

● Subtracting 3-Digit Numbers

## TEST-TAKING PRACTICE

Choose the best answer for each question.

346 Balloons

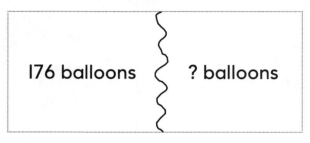

**1. Which question is shown by the diagram?**

A Nat had 176 balloons. He got 346 balloons. How many did he sell?

B Nat had 346 balloons. He sold 176 of them. How many were left over?

C Nat sold 176 balloons. He got 346 more balloons. How many did he sell in all?

D Not given

**2.** Seth had 317 prizes to give away. Each of the 137 winners got a prize. How many prizes were not given away?

J 137          L 317

K 180          M 454

**3.** Lily counted 173 bass drums and 348 snare drums. How many drums did she count?

A 175          C 421

B 348          D 521

**4.** The Bike Club had 575 safety lights to sell. They sold 342 of them. How many lights are there now?

J 342          L 233

K 917          M Not given

## Write About It

**5. Write the steps you would follow to solve this problem:**

Luz collects stickers. There are spaces for 800 stickers in her sticker book. She has filled 729 of the spaces with stickers. How many more stickers does she need to fill the book?

_____

_____

1. A ☐  B ☐  C ☐  D ☐     3. A ☐  B ☐  C ☐  D ☐

2. J ☐  K ☐  L ☐  M ☐     4. J ☐  K ☐  L ☐  M ☐

● Subtracting 3-Digit Numbers

# Using Counters to Choose the Operation

You can use counters to help you decide whether to add or multiply to solve a problem.

**Example:** Sally buys 3 sand dollars.
Sid buys a sea star, a sand dollar, and a shell.
Who pays more?

**A.** Look at the sign to find out how much each one pays.

**B.** Use counters to show how many cents each one pays.

**Sally**

There are the same number of counters in each row.

**So, you can multiply:**

5 x 3 = __15__

**Or you can add:**

5 + 5 + 5 = __15__

**How much does Sally pay?**

Sally pays __15¢__.

**Sid**

There are not the same number of counters in each row.

So, you cannot multiply:

**You can add:**

6 + 5 + 4 = __15__

**How much does Sid pay?**

Sid pays __15¢__.

**Answer the question:** __They pay the same amount__.

# GUIDED PRACTICE

1. Lark put 3 red shells and 4 black shells in her pail. Then she put in 5 white shells that Kim gave her. How many shells are in the pail?

   **Step 1:** Use counters to show the groups. Decide if you can multiply.

   **Step 2:** Write a number sentence to solve.

   **Answer the question:**

   There are _____ in the pail.

2. At the shell shop Cass bought 3 shells for 6¢ each. How much does she pay?

   **Step 1:** Use counters to show the groups. Decide if you can multiply.

   **Step 2:** Write a number sentence to solve.

   **Answer the question:**

   Cass pays _____.

Name _____

## PRACTICE

Use counters to show the problem. Write and
solve a number sentence.

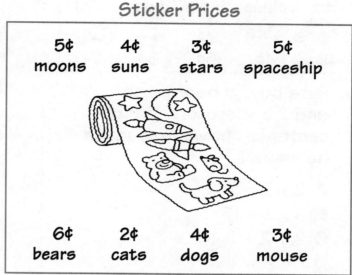

Sticker Prices

| 5¢ moons | 4¢ suns | 3¢ stars | 5¢ spaceship |
| 6¢ bears | 2¢ cats | 4¢ dogs | 3¢ mouse |

1. Lara buys a moon sticker,
   a cat sticker and a dog
   sticker. How much does
   she spend?

   _____

   Lara spends _____.

2. Omar buys 3 sun stickers
   and 2 dog stickers. How
   much does he spend?

   _____

   Omar spends _____.

3. Ellie buys 3 cat stickers and 2 dog stickers.
   How much does she spend?

   _____

   Ellie spends _____.

4. Jake buys 2 mouse stickers and 3 star stickers.

   _____

   Jake spends _____.

5. Yusuf buys 4 star stickers and a space ship
   sticker. He buys a bear sticker for his sister.
   How much does he spend?

   _____

   Yusuf spends _____.

● Multiplication Concepts

# TEST-TAKING PRACTICE

Choose the best answer for each problem.

Eraser Prices

car 6¢  plane 4¢  boat 5¢  bus 5¢  bike 7¢

**1.** Pete buys a boat eraser and 2 bus erasers. **Which sentence shows how much he spent?**

**A** 2 x 5 = 10
**B** 3 x 5 = 15
**C** 2 + 2 + 2 + 2 + 2 = 10
**D** 1 + 2 = 3

**2.** Leo buys 2 cars and 2 planes. Cassie buys 5 boats. **Who spends the most?**

**J** Leo
**K** Cassie
**L** They spend the same amount
**M** Not given

**3.** Cathy packs 4 car erasers in one gift box. She makes 4 boxes. **How many car erasers does she pack?**

**A** 4 boxes
**B** 8 car erasers
**C** 16 boxes
**D** 16 car erasers

**4.** Kobi gives 3 erasers to Jim. He gives 2 erasers to Jenna and 1 eraser to Max. All the erasers are planes. How much did Kobi spend on the gifts in all? **Choose the sentence that tells the story.**

**J** 3 + 2 + 1 = 6
**K** 6 + 6 + 6 + 6 + 6 + 6 = 36
**L** 6 x 3 = 18
**M** 6 x 4 = 24

## Write About It

**5.** Sara wants to buy 5 different color beads. Each bead costs the same amount. If she knows how many beads she wants in all, can she multiply to find out the total cost? **Explain how you would solve this problem.**

_____

_____

1. A ☐  B ☐  C ☐  D ☐       3. A ☐  B ☐  C ☐  D ☐

2. J ☐  K ☐  L ☐  M ☐       4. J ☐  K ☐  L ☐  M ☐

● Multiplication Concepts

# Using Skip-Counting to Multiply

You can solve some problems by skip-counting.

**Example:** Margo wants to make 4 owl puppets with button eyes. Each puppet has 2 eyes. How many buttons does she need?

**A.** To find out the number of buttons, she can count each one:

**1, 2,**          **3, 4,**          **5, 6,**          **7, 8**

**B.** She can also skip-count by 2 to find out how many buttons she needs. When you skip-count you only say some of the numbers. Skip-count the puppets' eyes.

think 1, **say 2**     think 3, **say 4**     think 5, **say 6**     think 7, **say 8**

**2**                    **4**                    **6**                    **8**

**Answer the question:** Margo needs ___8 buttons___.

## GUIDED PRACTICE

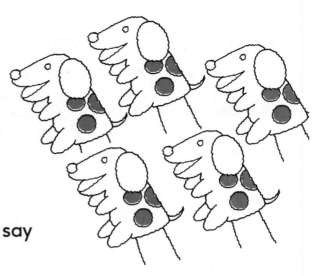

1. Jody made 5 dog puppets.
   Each puppet has 3 spots.
   How many spots did he make?

   **Step 1:** What number do you
   skip-count by?

   _____

   **Step 2:** Write the numbers you say
   as you skip-count.

   _____

   **Answer the question:** Jody made _____.

2. There are 6 people in the sticker club. They each give
   Lee 5 stickers. How many stickers does Lee get?

   **Step 1:** What number do you skip-count by?

   _____

   **Step 2:** Write the numbers you say as you skip-count.

   _____

   **Answer the question:** Lee gets _____.

3. Ellie puts 4 star stickers on each storybook. She has
   28 star stickers. How many storybooks have stickers?

   **Step 1:** What number do you skip-count by?

   _____

   **Step 2:** Write the numbers you say as you
   skip-count. Then count how many you wrote.

   _____

   **Answer the question:** ____ storybooks have stickers.

Name _____

## PRACTICE
Skip-count to find the answers.

1.  Jake has a rock collection. He puts the rocks in
    7 groups. Each group has 3 rocks in it. How many
    rocks does he have in all?

    skip-count by: _____

    Jake has _____ rocks in all.

2.  Jake's brother gives him more rocks and a new
    box for his collection. Each drawer holds 5 rocks.
    If he has 45 rocks, how many drawers does he fill?

    skip-count by: _____

    He fills _____ drawers.

3.  Bonnie collects shells. She has 32 shells.
    If she can keep all of them in 4 dishes,
    how many go in each dish?

    skip-count by: _____

    Bonnie puts _____ shells in each dish.

4.  Myra, Bill, and Jenny each made 6 magnets to
    sell. How many magnets did they make in all?

    skip-count by: _____

    They made _____ magnets in all.

5.  Jenny makes refrigerator magnets with shells.
    She glues 2 on each magnet. How many magnets
    can she make with 16 shells?

    skip-count by: _____

    Jenny can make _____ magnets.

© 1999 Metropolitan Teaching & Learning Co.

● Multiplication Concepts

# TEST-TAKING PRACTICE

Choose the best answer for each problem.

**1.** Ned put 3 stones in each box. He has 12 stones. How many boxes does he use? **What number would you skip-count by?**

**A** 2          **C** 4

**B** 3          **D** 12

**2.** Ken put his marbles in 6 bags. He put 4 marbles in each bag. **How many marbles does he have?**

**J** 6 marbles

**K** 10 marbles

**L** 24 marbles

**M** Not given

**3.** Sue has a bag of 14 apples. She wants to put 2 apples in each lunch bag. **How many lunch bags will she need?**

**A** 2 bags          **C** 14 bags

**B** 7 bags          **D** 30 bags

**4.** Nancy put 3 shells on each shelf. She put shells on 4 shelves. How many shells did she use? **Which list shows how you skip-count to find the answer?**

**J** 3, 6, 9, 12

**K** 4, 8, 12

**L** 1, 2, 3, 4

**M** 3, 4, 5, 6

## Write About It

**5.** Molly made 3 batches of cupcakes. Each batch has 12 cupcakes. How many cupcakes did she make? **Explain how you would solve this problem.**

_____

_____

1. A ☐  B ☐  C ☐  D ☐      3. A ☐  B ☐  C ☐  D ☐

2. J ☐  K ☐  L ☐  M ☐      4. J ☐  K ☐  L ☐  M ☐

© 1999 Metropolitan Teaching & Learning Co.

● Multiplication Concepts

# Using a Table

You can make a table to help solve a multiplication problem.

**Example:** Pat filled 9 bags with beads. He put 8 beads in a bag. How many beads did he use?

**A.** Make a table with 2 rows. The top row shows the bags. Label the row.

**How many bags does Pat use?** _9 bags_

| bags | 1 | 2 | 3 | 4 | 5 | 6 | 7 | 8 | 9 |
|------|---|---|---|---|---|---|---|---|---|

**B.** The second row shows the beads. Label the row.

**How many beads in a bag?** _8 beads_

**How many beads in 2 bags?** _16 beads_

| bags | 1 | 2 | 3 | 4 | 5 | 6 | 7 | 8 | 9 | ← row 1 |
|-------|----|----|----|----|----|----|----|----|----|---------|
| beads | 8 | 16 | 24 | 32 | 40 | 48 | 56 | 64 | 72 | ← row 2 |

**C.** Complete the table.

**Answer the question:** Pat used _72 beads_.

## GUIDED PRACTICE

Ted made a table to show how many beads he will need for 6 belts. He plans to use 8 beads for each belt.

Complete Ted's table.

| belt | 1 | 2 | ___ | ___ | ___ | 6 |
|------|---|---|-----|-----|-----|---|
| beads | 8 | ___ | ___ | ___ | 40 | ___ |

1. How many beads are there in 4 belts? _____

2. How many belts did Ted make with 24 beads? _____

3. How many beads did Ted use for all 6 belts? _____

4. Matt and Ann are planting tulips. They put 6 tulip bulbs in each flower bed. How many beds can they plant if they have 42 bulbs?

   Step 1: Make a table. Label the rows.

   Step 2: Complete the table

| ___ | ___ | ___ | ___ | ___ | ___ | ___ |
|-----|-----|-----|-----|-----|-----|-----|
| ___ | ___ | ___ | ___ | ___ | ___ | ___ |

   Answer the question: They can plant _____ .

## PRACTICE

Patsy made a table to figure out how many tires there are on 7 cars.

| cars | 1 | __ | __ | 4 | __ | 6 | __ |
|------|---|----|----|----|----|----|----|
| tires | 4 | __ | 12 | __ | 20 | __ | __ |

1. Complete the table. Then use it to answer the questions.

2. How many tires do 6 cars have? _____

3. Patsy counted 8 tires. How many cars were there? _____

4. Patsy counted 10 tires. She thinks she counted wrong. Why?

   _____

Make a table to solve the problem.

5. Ben puts 7 stickers on each page in his book.

   He has 42 stickers. How many pages he will use? _____

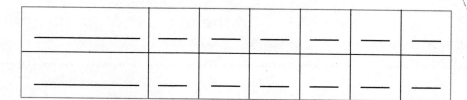

6. One box holds 3 tennis balls. Lisa counts 9 boxes on the shelf. How many tennis balls are there in all?

   _____

# TEST-TAKING PRACTICE

Choose the best answer for each problem.

| team | 1 | 2 | 3 | 4 | 5 |
|------|----|----|----|----|----|
| sandwich | 12 | 24 | ___ | 48 | 60 |

**1.** Peg made this table to find out how many sandwiches she needed for the picnic. **What number is missing from the table?**

**A** 30   **C** 72

**B** 36   **D** Not given

**2.** Sandy put 6 marbles in each bag. He has 9 bags. **How many marbles does he have?**

**J** 9 bags

**K** 15 marbles

**L** 54 marbles

**M** 60 marbles

**3.** John made up 7 gift bags. He put 3 magnets, a yo-yo, and a ball in each bag. **How many magnets did he use?**

**A** 10 bags

**B** 21 magnets

**C** 21 bags

**D** 49 magnets

**4.** Kate made 3 sandwiches for each member of her team. **What do you need to know to make a table to find out how many sandwiches Kate made?**

**J** the number of teams in the league

**K** the number of sandwiches each person eats

**L** the number of sandwiches she can make in an hour

**M** the number of people on Kate's team

## Write About It

**5.** Sam put 6 beads on each belt. If Sam made 4 belts and had 3 beads left over, how many beads did he have to start? **Explain how you got your answer.**

_____

_____

1. A☐  B☐  C☐  D☐     3. A☐  B☐  C☐  D☐
2. J☐  K☐  L☐  M☐     4. J☐  K☐  L☐  M☐

● Multiplication Concepts

# Deciding What to Do First

You might have to do more than one operation to solve some problems. Start by deciding what to do first.

**Example:** Petra can make 2 rings in an hour. She works 3 hours every day. How many rings can she make in 4 days?

**A. Which is easier to find out?** Underline one.

- <u>how many rings she makes in 1 day</u>

- how many rings she makes in 4 days

**B.** First, multiply to find how many rings Petra makes in 1 day.

Write a word sentence and a number sentence.

<u>Rings in 1 hour</u> x <u>Hours</u> = <u>Total rings a day</u>

___2___ x ___3___ = ___6___

**How many rings can Petra make each day?** ___6 rings___

**C.** Now, multiply to find out how many rings Petra can make in 4 days.

Write a word sentence and a number sentence.

<u>Rings in 1 day</u> x <u>Days</u> = <u>Total rings</u>

___6___ x ___4___ = ___24___

**Answer the question:** Petra can make ___24 rings___ in 4 days.

## GUIDED PRACTICE

1. Ben can paint 3 bookmarks in an hour. He paints for 3 hours each day. How many bookmarks can he paint in 5 days?

   **Step 1:** Decide what to find out first. Underline one.

   - how many bookmarks in 5 days

   - how many bookmarks in 1 day

   **Step 2:** Multiply to find out how many bookmarks he can paint in 1 day.

   Write a word sentence and a number sentence.

   _____ x _____ = _____

   _____

   **Ben can paint _____ each day.**

   **Step 3:** Multiply to find out how many bookmarks he can paint in 5 days.

   _____ x _____ = _____

   _____

   **Answer the question:** Ben can paint _____ in 5 days.

2. Omar fed the 3 goats in the petting zoo 3 times a day. He gave each goat 2 carrots at each feeding. How many carrots did Omar use in 1 day?

   **Step 1:** Decide what to find out first.

   **Step 2:** Multiply to find out how many carrots

   for each feeding . _____

   **Step 3:** Multiply to find out how many carrots

   for all 3 feedings. _____

   **Answer the question:** Omar used _____ in 1 day.

© 1999 Metropolitan Teaching & Learning Co.

Name _____

## PRACTICE

**1.** Lynn made lunch for her 4 little brothers. She cut 2 carrot sticks to put in each lunch bag. She made lunch 5 days a week. How many carrot sticks did Lynn make in a week?

_____

Lynn made _____.

**2.** Bob's Bakery uses 3 apples to make 1 apple tart. They make 2 tarts an hour. How many apples do they use in 7 hours?

_____

Bob's Bakery uses _____ in 7 hours.

**3.** Sally's Deli packs 2 pickles with every sandwich. They sold 5 sandwiches an hour for 4 hours in a row. How many pickles did they use in all?

_____

Sally's Deli used _____ in all.

**4.** Kelly sold 4 glasses of orange juice on Monday. She sold the same number of glasses on Tuesday and Friday. She squeezed 2 oranges for each glass. How many oranges did she squeeze on those 3 days?

_____

She squeezed _____.

**5.** Greg plans to make 2 pies for each of his 3 cousins. He will need 4 cups of blueberries for each pie. How many cups will he need for all of the pies?

_____

He will need _____ of blueberries.

● Multiplication Concepts

# TEST-TAKING PRACTICE

Choose the best answer for each problem.

**I.** Kim wants to make 2 scarves for each of her 4 friends. Each scarf will use 5 balls of yarn. **How many balls of yarn should she get?**

**A** 8 scarves

**B** 40 scarves

**C** 40 balls of yarn

**D** 80 balls of yarn

**2.** There are 5 passengers on each of 6 boats. Each passenger has 2 suitcases. **How many suitcases are on all of the boats?**

**J** 12 suitcases

**K** 30 passengers

**L** 60 passengers

**M** 60 suitcases

**3.** There are 2 cupcakes on each tray. There are 2 trays. Dave wants to put 3 candles on top of each cupcake. **How many candles does he need?**

**A** 7 candles

**B** 12 candles

**C** 12 cupcakes

**D** not given

**4.** Olga wants to give I ball to 5 winners each day. **How many balls does she need to give to winners for 3 days?**

**J** 5 balls

**K** 8 balls

**L** 10 balls

**M** 15 balls

## Write About It

**5.** Jim wants to make 3 hats for each of his sisters. He will use 2 balls of yarn for each hat. He has 3 sisters. How much yarn does he need? What would you find out first to solve this problem? **Explain your choice, then solve.**

_____

_____

_____

1. A ☐  B ☐  C ☐  D ☐

2. J ☐  K ☐  L ☐  M ☐

3. A ☐  B ☐  C ☐  D ☐

4. J ☐  K ☐  L ☐  M ☐

# Test-Taking Skill: Writing a Plan

Some questions on tests ask you to explain how you solve a problem. You can write a plan to show the steps you take to find the answer.

**Example:** Pat has $17.85. Then he buys a book for $7.99 and a box of markers for $5.50. How much money does he have left?

**A.** **To solve this problem, you will need to do more than one operation. Decide what the answer will be.**

The answer will be an amount of money.

**Decide what you have to do to solve the problem.**

You can add and then subtract or you can subtract two times.

**B.** **Write a plan for finding the answer. You can number the steps you will take.**

**1.** Find how much Pat spent on the book and markers.

**2.** Add to find the total amount Pat spent.

**3.** Subtract the total from $17.85 to find how much change he got.

**C.** Follow your plan to solve. Show your calculations.

**1.** $7.99 for the book; $5.50 for the markers

**2.**     7.99
        +   5.50
        _____

**3.**     17.85
          −
        _____

**D.** Answer the question: Pat has _____ left.

# TEST-TAKING PRACTICE

Write a plan to solve each problem. Follow the steps of your plan.

1. Hetty spends 3 hours a day making muffins. She can bake 12 muffins an hour. How many muffins can she make in 5 days?

   **Step 1:** Write a plan. Choose the easiest way for you to find the answer. Number the steps.

   _____

   _____

   _____

   _____

   _____

   _____

   **Step 2:** Follow your plan.

   _____

   _____

   _____

   **Answer the question:**

   She makes _____ in 5 days.

2. Sandy made 3 sandwiches for each person at her party. She invited 6 people. Each sandwich used 2 slices of bread. How many slices did she cut?

   **Step 1:** Write a plan.

   _____

   _____

   _____

   _____

   _____

   _____

   _____

   _____

   **Step 2:** Follow your plan.

   _____

   _____

   _____

   **Answer the question:**

   Sandy cut _____ of bread.

Name _____

# Making a Diagram

You can make a diagram to help solve problems about making equal groups.

**Example 1:** Ben found 30 stones. He puts 6 stones in a bag. How many bags does he use for all of the stones?

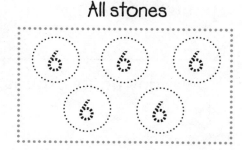

All stones

**A.** Decide what you know and what you need to find out.

**Do you know how many in each group?** ___yes___

**Do you know how many groups?** ___no___

**B.** Draw and label a box to stand for all the stones.

How many stones will be in each bag? ___6 stones___

**C.** For each group of 6 stones, write a 6 inside the box and draw a circle around it.

Skip-count by 6 until you get to 30. Then count the circles.

**Answer the question:** Ben uses ___5 bags___.

**Example 2:** Mia has 12 stones. She divided them equally among 4 bags. How many stones are in each bag?

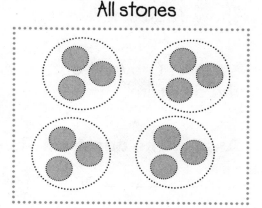

All stones

**Step 1:** Decide what you know and what you need to find out. Draw 4 circles to stand for the 4 bags.

**Step 2:** Draw one dot for each stone. Go from circle to circle, until you have drawn 12 dots in all. Count the number of dots in one circle to find how many stones are in each bag.

**Answer the question:** There are ___3 stones___ in each bag.

● Division Facts

## GUIDED PRACTICE

Use the diagram to answer the questions.

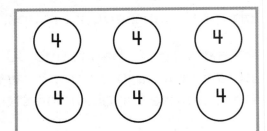

1. How many beads are in each equal group?

_____

2. How many equal groups of beads are there?

_____

3. By what number would you skip-count to find how many beads there are in all?

_____

4. Joan made 8 necklaces and used 24 red beads in all. She used the same number of red beads for each necklace. How many red beads are on each necklace?

**Step 1:** The circles in the diagram show Joan's necklaces.

**Step 2:** Draw 24 dots to complete the diagram.

**Answer the question:** There are

_____ on each necklace.

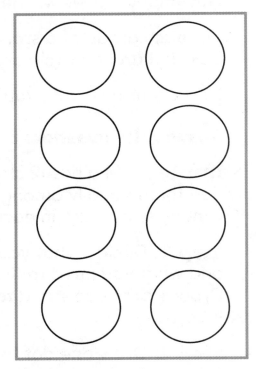

## PRACTICE

Draw a diagram to help you solve each problem.

**1.** There were 36 people at the Adventure Club picnic. If I bottle of juice holds enough to serve 4 people, how many bottles of juice were needed?

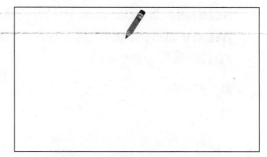

_____

**2.** The people at the picnic ate 56 hamburgers on buns. The cook used up 7 packages of buns. How many buns were in each package?

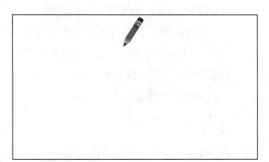

_____

**3.** Keshawn sold adventure caps to raise money for the picnic. He sold each cap for $5. He raised $45. How many caps did he sell?

_____

**4.** Luisa sold 7 adventure tote bags. She raised $49 for the picnic. What was the cost of each tote bag?

_____

**5.** The club goes on an adventure trip 6 times a year. Each trip takes the same amount of time. If the club spent a total of 24 hours on their trips last year, how much time did I trip take?

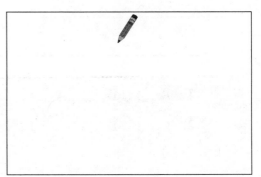

_____

● Division Facts

## TEST-TAKING PRACTICE

Choose the best answer for each problem.

**1. If Yola reads 5 pages in her science book each day, how many days will it take her to read 35 pages?**

**A** 3     **C** 7

**B** 5     **D** 35

**2.** Max returned a book to the library. It was 4 days overdue. He paid a fine of 20¢. **How much does the library charge per day for an overdue book?**

**J** 2¢     **L** 5¢

**K** 4¢     **M** 20¢

**3.** Yola checks her bird feeder the same number of times each day. In 7 days she checked the feeder 42 times. **How many times did she check it each day?**

**A** 6     **C** 35

**B** 7     **D** Not given

**4.** Max chose a book for his report. The book has 56 pages. He wants to read the same number of pages each day for 7 days. **How many pages should he read each day to finish the book?**

**J** 5     **L** 7

**K** 6     **M** 8

## Write About It

**5. Tell how you would solve this problem:**

There are 4 players in a game. Each player gets the same number of cards. There are 52 cards in all. **How many cards does each player get?**

_____

_____

_____

1. A ☐  B ☐  C ☐  D ☐      3. A ☐  B ☐  C ☐  D ☐

2. J ☐  K ☐  L ☐  M ☐      4. J ☐  K ☐  L ☐  M ☐

● Division Facts

# Finding Needed Information

Sometimes it helps to organize the information in a problem before you try to solve it.

**Example 1:** Mary and her 2 brothers found 12 pumpkins in a pumpkin patch. If they share the pumpkins equally, how many pumpkins will each get?

**A.** Decide what you know and what you need to find out.

Ring yes or no. Then write the answer if you know it.

| | | |
|---|---|---|
| **How many pumpkins in all?** | (yes) no | 12 pumpkins |
| **How many people?** | (yes) no | 3 people |
| **How many pumpkins will each person get?** | yes (no) | |

**B.** Divide to find how many in each equal group. ___12 ÷ 3 = 4___

**Answer the question:** Each person will get ___4 pumpkins___.

**Example 2:** Linda picked 35 apples. She gave 5 apples to each friend and kept 5 apples for herself. How many people shared the apples?

**Step 1:** Decide what you know and what you need to find out.

Write yes or no. Then, write the answer if you know it.

**How many apples in all?** ___yes___     ___35 apples___

**How many people got apples?** ___no___

**How many apples did each person get?** ___yes___  ___5 apples___

**Step 2:** Divide to find the number of people. ___35 ÷ 5 = 7___

**Answer the question:** ___7 people___ shared the apples.

## GUIDED PRACTICE

Organize the information in each problem
before you try to solve it.

1. Seth has 28 party favors. He puts
   4 favors into each favor bag.
   How many favor bags are there?

   **Step 1:** Decide what you know
   and what you need to find out.

   Ring what you know.

   - Number of favors in all

   - Number of bags

   - Number in each bag

   **Step 2:** Write and solve a division sentence.

   _____

   **Answer the question:** There are _____ favor bags.

2. Rachel paid 72¢ for
   8 pencils. How much
   did each pencil cost?

   **Step 1:** Decide what
   you know and what
   you need to find out.

   Ring what you know.

   - Total cost

   - Number of pencils

   - Cost of each pencil

   These words can help you organize
   information in a division problem
   about money.

   **Total** is the **total cost.**
   **Number of groups** is the **number
   of items bought.**
   **Number in each group** is the
   **cost of each item.**

   **Step 2:** Write and solve a division sentence.

   _____

   **Answer the question:** Each pencil cost _____.

© 1999 Metropolitan Teaching & Learning Co.

## PRACTICE

**1.** Joe's Sports sells golf balls for $9 per box. Ed bought $45 worth of golf balls. How many boxes did he buy?

_____ Ed bought _____ boxes.

**2.** Charles went to the art store. He bought 42 markers. There were 7 markers in each package. How many packages did he buy?

_____ Charles bought _____.

**3.** Sam's family went to the movies. They paid $40 for tickets. Each ticket cost $8. How many people are in Sam's family?

_____ There are _____ in Sam's family.

**4.** Ms. Thieu bought 6 cinnamon sticks. She paid 48¢ for them. What was the cost of each cinnamon stick?

_____ Each stick cost _____.

**5.** A clown gave away 24 balloons. He gave the same number of balloons to each of 6 children. How many balloons did he give to each child?

_____ He gave each child _____.

**6.** Mrs. Stevens bought 12 roses. She put an equal number of roses in 3 vases. How many roses did she put in each vase?

_____ She put _____ in each vase.

● Meanings of Division

## TEST-TAKING PRACTICE

Choose the best answer for each problem.

**1.** Ms. Kane's class worked on a mural for 2 hours every day. It took the class 18 hours to finish the mural. **How many days did the class work on it?**

**A** 9 hours    **C** 9 days
**B** 36 hours   **D** 18 days

**2.** A zoo book has a 5-page story about each animal. The book has 35 pages in all. **How many animals does the book have a story about?**

**J** 7        **L** 8
**K** 5       **M** 6

**3.** Mr. Martin's class brought in 63 cans of food for a food drive. The food drive lasted 7 days, and the same number of cans were brought in each day. **How many cans were brought in each day?**

**A** 7       **C** 9
**B** 8       **D** 63

**4.** Jackie set up 4 equal rows of chairs for a meeting. There were 32 chairs in all. **How many chairs were in each row?**

**J** 4       **L** 32
**K** 8      **M** Not given

## Write About It

**5.** There are 27 people in the club. They want to form equal groups to play a game. Explain different ways the 27 people can form equal groups. **Tell how many people there would be in each group, and how many groups there would be.**

_____

_____

| | | | |
|---|---|---|---|
| 1. A ☐ | B ☐ | C ☐ | D ☐ |
| 2. J ☐ | K ☐ | L ☐ | M ☐ |

| | | | |
|---|---|---|---|
| 3. A ☐ | B ☐ | C ☐ | D ☐ |
| 4. J ☐ | K ☐ | L ☐ | M ☐ |

● Meanings of Division

# Underlining Important Information

Sometimes a problem has more information than you need to solve it.

**Example 1:** There are 36 people going to the park. 12 of them are adults. If the van can take 9 people on each trip to the park, how many trips will it take to get everyone to the park?

**A.** Start by reading the problem carefully. **Underline the information you need to answer the question.**

There are 36 people going to the park. 12 of them are adults. If the van can take 9 people on each trip to the park, how many trips will it take to get everyone to the park?

**B. Write and solve a division sentence.** $36 \div 9 = 4$

**Answer the question:** It will take ___4 trips___ to get everyone to the park.

**Example 2:** At the park, 32 children formed teams for a game. There were 15 boys and 17 girls. All 4 teams had the same number of players. How many children were on each team?

**Step 1: Underline the information you need.**

At the park, 32 children formed teams for a game. There were 15 boys and 17 girls. All 4 teams had the same number of players. How many children were on each team?

**Step 2: Write and solve a division sentence.** $32 \div 4 = 8$

**Answer the question:** There were ___8 children___ on each team.

## GUIDED PRACTICE

1. Ring the letter of the problem that has the information you need underlined.

**IA** Tom has 54 tulip bulbs. 26 will be red tulips, and the other 28 will be yellow tulips. He plants 6 bulbs in each row. How many rows does he plant?

**IB** Tom has 54 tulip bulbs. 26 will be red tulips, and the other 28 will be yellow tulips. He plants 6 bulbs in each row. How many rows does he plant?

2. Ring the sentence that shows problem I.

$54 \div 6$          $54 - 28$          $26 + 28$          $54 \div 28$

3. Solve problem I. Then answer the question.

_____          He plants _____.

4. Jim's friends help him move the garden supplies. There are 27 boxes to move. Everyone carries 3 boxes. There are 17 big boxes and 10 little boxes. How many people helped carry the boxes?

**Step 1:** Underline the information you need.

**Step 2:** Write and solve a division sentence.

_____          _____ people helped.

## PRACTICE

**1.** There are 7 artists who make birthday cards. The card company sells 49 different birthday cards. 35 of the cards are funny, 10 are serious, and 4 are blank inside. Each artist makes the same number of cards. How many birthday cards does each artist make?

_____        _____

**2.** There are 12 singers in the song club. 7 singers are girls and 5 are boys. There are 94 songs in their song book. Each song takes 4 minutes to sing. The show will be 36 minutes long. What is the greatest number of songs they can sing during the show?

_____        _____

**3.** The band concert was 50 minutes long. There are 24 players who play horns. 12 of them have played for more than two years. If 3 horn players shared 1 music stand for the concert, how many music stands did the horn players use?

_____        _____

**4.** There are 7 jugglers in the show. Each one can juggle 3 balls or 5 clubs. During one act there were 18 balls in the air. How many jugglers were there?

_____        _____

**5.** There are 24 clowns in the show. 12 of the clowns have red noses. 8 of them are wearing big shoes. All the clowns squeeze into tiny cars at the end of the show. Each tiny car can hold 6 clowns. How many tiny cars do the clowns use?

_____        _____

# TEST-TAKING PRACTICE

Choose the best answer for each problem.

**1.** The 2 children played the Lily Pond game at the carnival. Each player gets 3 plastic frogs to play 1 game. Jeremy got 15 plastic frogs. Sue played 2 games. How many games did Jeremy play? **What information is not needed to solve the problem?**

**A** 3 plastic frogs
**B** Sue played 2 games
**C** 15 plastic frogs
**D** Not given

**2.** There are 45 people at the museum. Each guide leads a group of 9 people. The tours last for 1 hour. 36 people go on tours. **How many tour guides lead groups?**

**J** 4 hours
**K** 4 tour guides
**L** 5 tour guides
**M** 9 people

**3.** Mr. Long had $48 for snack money. He gave each person on the field trip $6 of the snack money to spend. Sodas cost $1 each and hot dogs cost $2 each. **How many people got money for snacks?**

**A** $3
**B** 8 people
**C** 6 people
**D** $2

## Write About It

**4. Describe how you solved problem 3 above.**

_____

_____

_____

_____

1. A ☐  B ☐  C ☐  D ☐    3. A ☐  B ☐  C ☐  D ☐
2. J ☐  K ☐  L ☐  M ☐

● Multiplication and Division

# Using a Table of Equivalent Measures

You can use a table to rename two measures with the same unit so you can compare them.

**Example:** Jenny bought 1 pint of cream. A cake recipe calls for 3 cups of cream. Does she have enough cream to make the cake?

**A.** Read the problem. **What units do you need to compare?**

___1___ pint  and  ___3___ cups

| Units of Capacity | |
|---|---|
| 1 pint | 2 cups |
| 1 quart | 2 pints |
| 1 gallon | 4 quarts |

**B.** You can use the table to find out how cups and pints are related.

Find cups and pints on the table.

Ring the measure that holds more:

• (pints)     • cups

**How many cups are there in 1 pint?**

Write a number sentence. ___2 cups = 1 pint___

**C.** Rename the amount of cream that Jenny has using the smaller unit.

**Jenny has 1 pint or ___2___ cups of cream.**

**D.** Compare the amount of cream Jenny has to the amount she needs using the same unit of measure.

**Jenny has ___2 cups___ of cream.**

**Jenny needs ___3 cups___ of cream.**

**Answer the question:** Does Jenny have enough cream to make the cake?

___no___

## GUIDED PRACTICE

Use the table to solve a problem.

1. Juan uses 2 ribbons for his art project. The red ribbon is 1 yard long. The blue ribbon is 2 feet long. Which ribbon is shorter?

**Step 1:** Find the information you need on the table. Ring the two measures you need to compare.

| Units of Length | |
|---|---|
| 1 foot | 12 inches |
| 1 yard | 3 feet |
| 1 mile | 1,760 yards |

• inches   • feet   • yards   • miles

Write a number sentence.

_____

**Step 2:** Rename the length of Juan's ribbons using the smaller unit.

**Juan's red ribbon is** _____.

Compare the length of the two ribbons using the same unit of measure.

The red ribbon is _____ .

The blue ribbon is _____.

**Answer the question:** _____ is shorter.

2. Tina ran 1,798 yards. Alex ran 1 mile. Who ran farther?

**Step 1:** Find the information you need on the table.

Write the number sentence.

_____

**Step 2:** Rename the distance using the smaller unit.

Compare the distance using the same unit of measure.

_____

**Answer the question:** Who ran farther? _____

## PRACTICE
Write the comparisons and answer the questions.

1.  Etsuko's thermos holds 12 fluid ounces. Mike's thermos holds 2 cups. Whose thermos holds more?

    _____

    _____

    _____ thermos holds more.

| Units of Capacity | |
|---|---|
| 1 cup | 8 fluid ounces |
| 1 pint | 2 cups |
| 1 quart | 2 pints |
| 1 gallon | 4 quarts |

2.  Luis needs 1 gallon of apple juice to make fruit punch. There are 5 quarts of apple juice on the shelf. Does he have enough?

    _____

    _____

3.  Carlos bought a 28-ounce can of tomato sauce. The pizza recipe calls for 1 pound of sauce. Does he have enough?

    _____

    _____

4.  Serena needs 1 pound of corn to make corn bread. The largest can in the store weighs 11 ounces. Does she need more than 1 can?

| Units of Weight | |
|---|---|
| 1 pound | 16 ounces |
| 1 ton | 2,000 pounds |

    _____

    _____

# TEST-TAKING PRACTICE

| Units of Length | |
|---|---|
| I foot | 12 inches |
| I yard | 36 inches |
| I yard | 3 feet |
| I mile | 5,280 feet |
| I mile | 1,760 yards |

**I.** Yuri used 5 feet of crepe paper. Kathy used I yard of crepe paper. Who used the most crepe paper? **Which two units do you compare?**

**A** feet and inches

**B** yards and miles

**C** feet and yards

**D** inches and yards

**2.** Luke uses I yard of ribbon. Tom uses 38 inches of ribbon. **Who uses the most ribbon?**

**J** Tom

**K** Luke

**L** Both use the same

**M** Not given

**3.** Judy glues a 3-foot strip of red paper to a strip of blue paper that is I yard long. **Which color strip is longer?**

**A** red

**B** blue

**C** Both are the same length

**D** 4 feet

**4. How many 18-inch strips of ribbon can Ann cut from a foot-long piece of ribbon?**

**J** I strip     **L** 18 strips

**K** 2 strips    **M** No strips

## Write About It

**5. Explain how you would solve this problem:** Carlos needs 20-ounces of peas for the recipe. He finds a package that holds I pound of peas. **Will he use the whole package?**

_____

_____

1. A ☐  B ☐  C ☐  D ☐      3. A ☐  B ☐  C ☐  D ☐

2. J ☐  K ☐  L ☐  M ☐      4. J ☐  K ☐  L ☐  M ☐

# Showing Information a Different Way

To solve problems that use measurement you can rename the measures. Sometimes you need to compute to make the units in a problem match.

**Example:** Kit has a bowl that can hold 8 cups of water. How many pints of water can he pour into the bowl?

**A.** Read the problem.
**What measures do you need to use?**

_____pints_____ and _____cups_____

Ring the one that holds a greater amount.

- I cup     - (I pint)

**How many cups are there in I pint?**
Write the number sentence.

_____I pint = 2 cups_____

**B.** You can find the answer by making a table that relates cups to pints.

First, make a table. Put the larger unit of measure in the top row.

| pints | 1 | 2 | 3 | 4 |
|-------|---|---|---|---|
| cups  | 2 | 4 | 6 | 8 |

**C.** Complete the table.

**Answer the question:** Kit can pour

_____4 pints of water_____ into the bowl.

## GUIDED PRACTICE

Make a table to answer the questions.

1.  Noe used a quart jar to pour water into the fish tank. The tank holds 5 gallons of water. How many quarts did he pour?

    **Step 1:** Make the table to find the answer. What units of measure will be shown on the table?

    _____

    Write the number sentence. _____

    | _____ | ___ | ___ | ___ | ___ | ___ |
    |---|---|---|---|---|---|
    | _____ | ___ | ___ | ___ | ___ | ___ |

    **Step 2:** Complete the table.

    **Answer the question:** Noe poured _____.

2.  Sarah made 18 pints of apple sauce. She measured it all into quart jars. How many jars did she fill?

    **Step 1:** Make the table to find the answer. What units of measure will be shown on the table?

    _____

    Write the number sentence. _____

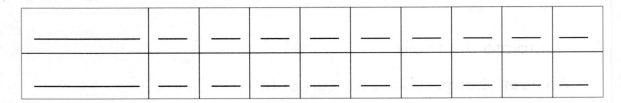

    **Step 2:** Complete the table.

    **Answer the question:** Sarah filled _____.

## PRACTICE
Make a table to find the answer.

1. Edgar says his computer weighs 64 ounces. Mike says his computer weighs 4 pounds. Whose computer weighs more?

|  |  |  |  |  |  |  |  |
|---|---|---|---|---|---|---|---|
|  |  |  |  |  |  |  |  |

2. Fran's dog weighs 7 pounds. Jan's cat weighs 128 ounces. Does Jan's cat weigh more or less than Fran's dog?

|  |  |  |  |  |  |  |  |
|---|---|---|---|---|---|---|---|
|  |  |  |  |  |  |  |  |

3. Hilda made 7 gallons of strawberry syrup. She put it into quart jars. How many jars did she fill?

|  |  |  |  |  |  |  |  |
|---|---|---|---|---|---|---|---|
|  |  |  |  |  |  |  |  |

4. Bill needs 22 feet of wire for his model. The roll of wire has 6 yards on it. Will he have enough?

|  |  |  |  |  |  |  |  |
|---|---|---|---|---|---|---|---|
|  |  |  |  |  |  |  |  |

5. Piers poured 72 glasses of juice at the school picnic. Each glass held 1 pint. How many gallons of juice did he use?

|  |  |  |  |  |  |  |  |
|---|---|---|---|---|---|---|---|
|  |  |  |  |  |  |  |  |

# TEST-TAKING PRACTICE

Choose the best answer for each problem.

**1.** A baker used 6 gallons of water to make bread this morning. **How many quarts of water did he use?**

**A** 6 quarts    **C** 24 quarts
**B** 12 quarts    **D** 3 quarts

**2.** Toya measured the length of a hallway. It was 24 feet long. **How many yards long was it?**

**J** 2 yards    **L** 12 yards
**K** 8 yards    **M** 72 yards

**3.** Robert caught a fish that weighed 144 ounces. **How many pounds did it weigh?**

**A** 1 pound    **C** 9 pounds
**B** 5 pounds    **D** 100 pounds

**4.** Jessica used 7 cans of beans to make soup. Each can held 16 ounces of beans. **How many pounds of beans did she use?**

**J** 7 pounds    **L** 64 pounds
**K** 16 pounds    **M** 112 ounces

**5.** **Which measure could you write in the empty space to make the table true?**

| gallons | 1 | 2 | 3 |
|---------|---|---|----|
| ? | 4 | 8 | 12 |

**A** cups    **C** ounces
**B** pints    **D** quarts

## Write About It

**6. Describe how you would solve this problem:** The ice-cream maker made an 8-gallon tub of vanilla ice cream. How many 1-pint containers can he fill?

_____

_____

1. A ☐   B ☐   C ☐   D ☐     4. J ☐   K ☐   L ☐   M ☐

2. J ☐   K ☐   L ☐   M ☐     5. A ☐   B ☐   C ☐   D ☐

3. A ☐   B ☐   C ☐   D ☐

● Measurement

# Using a Line Graph

A line graph shows how something changes over time.

**Example:** Ling planted a pea plant on June 1. Every Friday, he measured the plant. He made this line graph to show how much the pea plant grew from June 1 to June 22.

**A.** The labels on the bottom of the graph show when Ling recorded his measurements.

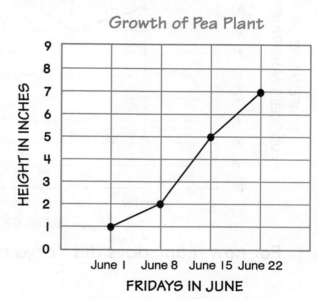

**How many times did Ling measure the plant?**

_4 times_

The numbers on the left side of the graph show how tall the plant was. **What unit of measure did Ling use?**

_inches_

**B.** The points on the graph show how tall the plant was each time Ling measured. Find the point on the line labeled June 1. Now read across to the left to find the height.

**How tall was the plant on June 1?** _1 inch tall_

**C.** The lines that connect the points on the graph make it easier to see how the height changed.

**Did the plant grow taller between June 15 and June 22?**

_yes_

Count the upward spaces between the points.

**How many inches did the plant grow between June 15 and June 22?**

_2 inches_

● Measurement

## GUIDED PRACTICE

Katya wrote down the temperature every day at the same time. Then she made this line graph to show the information.

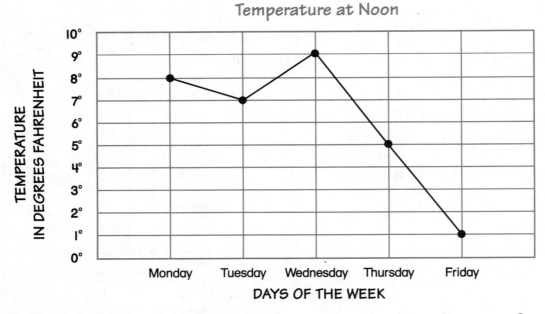

**Temperature at Noon**

1. For how many days did Katya record the temperature?

   _____

2. What unit of measurement did she use?

   _____

3. Was it colder on Monday or on Friday?

   _____

4. What was the temperature at noon on the

   day that was warmest? _____

5. How much colder was it at noon on Thursday than on Wednesday?

   **Step 1:** Find Wednesday and Thursday at the bottom of the graph.

   **Step 2:** Read up to the points. Then count the spaces between the points.

   **Answer the question: It was _____.**

## PRACTICE

Use the line graph to answer the questions.

The kitten was born on March 3. Lars weighed it on the third of the month for the next 3 months. He made this line graph to show how much the kitten grew.

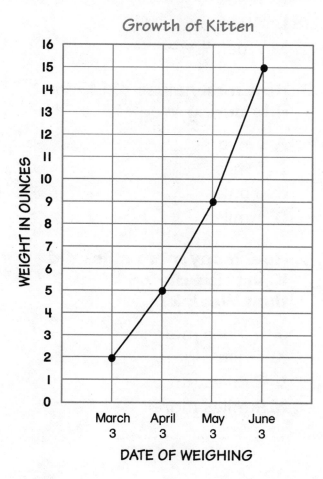

Growth of Kitten

WEIGHT IN OUNCES

DATE OF WEIGHING

**1.** For how many months did Lars weigh the kitten?

_____

**2.** How much did the kitten weigh on March 3?

_____

**3.** How much did the kitten weigh on June 3?

_____

**4.** Did the kitten grow every month?

_____

**5.** Did the kitten grow the same amount every month?

_____

**6.** The kitten was born on March 3. How much did it weigh when it was 2 months old?

_____

**7.** How much did the kitten grow between March 3 and April 3?

_____

**8.** How much did the kitten grow between March 3 and June 3?

_____

## TEST-TAKING PRACTICE

Choose the best answer for each problem.

**How Far Kevin Rode His Bike**

DISTANCE IN MILES

Week 1  Week 2  Week 3  Week 4

WEEKS IN JULY

**1. What is the graph about?**

**A** how many miles Kevin ran each week in July

**B** how far Kevin rides his bike each day

**C** how many miles Kevin rode his bike each week in July

**D** how many weeks Kevin rode his bike

**2. Which week did Kevin ride the most miles?**

**J** Week 1

**K** Week 2

**L** Week 3

**M** Week 4

**3. How many miles did Kevin ride during Week 1?**

**A** 1 mile

**B** 3 miles

**C** 6 miles

**D** 7 miles

**4. How many more miles did Kevin ride during Week 3 than Week 2?**

**J** 0 miles more

**K** 1 mile more

**L** 2 miles more

**M** 4 miles more

## Write About It

**5.** How much farther did Kevin ride in Week 4 than in Week 2? **Explain how you would solve the problem, and then solve.**

_____

_____

1. A☐  B☐  C☐  D☐      3. A☐  B☐  C☐  D☐

2. J☐  K☐  L☐  M☐      4. J☐  K☐  L☐  M☐

● Measurement

## Test-Taking Skill:
# Try Showing the Problem a Different Way

If you have trouble understanding a problem, try showing it a different way. Here are some ideas.

- Make a diagram or drawing
- Use counters

- Write a word sentence
- Make a table

**Example 1:** Angie needs 5 cups of water. Her bottle holds 3 pints. Does she have enough?

***THINK:*** I have to rename pints as cups. I can **make a table** to find out how many cups are in 3 pints.

**A** 3 cups          **B** no          **C** yes          **D** 6 pints

**Example 2:** Avi separates his 176 basketball and baseball cards. He has 96 baseball cards. How many basketball cards does he have?

***THINK:*** I know the number in the whole set and how many are in one part of the whole set. I can **draw a diagram** to see what I need to do to find the answer.

**J** 20          **K** 96          **L** 80          **M** 176

**Example 3:** Pete can paint 4 boxes in an hour. He can paint for 3 hours every day.  How many boxes can he paint in 6 days?

***THINK:*** I have to multiply twice. I can **write a word sentence** to make the steps clear.

**A** 7 boxes          **B** 12 boxes          **C** 24 boxes          **D** 72 boxes

1. A ☐  B ☐  C ☐  D ☐          3. A ☐  B ☐  C ☐  D ☐

2. J ☐  K ☐  L ☐  M ☐

# TEST-TAKING PRACTICE

Show each problem another way to help you solve the problem.

**1.** Lia wants to make fruit punch. The recipe calls for 8 cups of apple juice. The juice is sold in pint jars. **How many jars does she need?**

**A** 4 pints     **C** 16 cups
**B** 8 pints     **D** 16 pints

**2.** Joelle has 60 beads. She can put 5 beads in each drawer. **How many drawers does she fill?**

**J** 5         **L** 60
**K** 12       **M** 300

**3.** There are 749 seats in the theater. The balcony has 235 seats. **How many seats are on the main floor?**

**A** 235     **C** 749
**B** 514     **D** 984

**4.** Jackie bought 5 red stones for 6¢ each. Mona bought 2 black stones for 5¢ each, 1 white stone for 5¢, and 3 green stones for 4¢ each. **Who paid more?**

**J** Mona paid more.
**K** Jackie paid less.
**L** Jackie paid more.
**M** They paid the same amount.

**5.** Bogdan buys a book for $3.27 and a toy car for $2.25. **How much does he spend on both?**

**A** $2.25     **C** $5.00
**B** $3.27     **D** $5.52

1. A☐ B☐ C☐ D☐     4. J☐ K☐ L☐ M☐
2. J☐ K☐ L☐ M☐     5. A☐ B☐ C☐ D☐
3. A☐ B☐ C☐ D☐

# Using a Map

To solve some problems, you may have to find information by reading a map.

**Example:** Lara goes to the Post Office from her house. Then she goes to the Fairgrounds. She passes Town Hall on her way. How far does she travel?

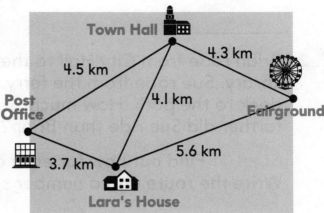

**A.** Find the places on the map named in the problem. Use your finger to trace the route Lara takes from her house to the Fairgrounds.

**B.** The distance between one point on the map and the next is found in the label on the line between the points. **How far is it from Lara's house to the Post Office?**

_____3.7 kilometers_____

**C.** Write the words to show the route Lara takes. Then write the distances between each stop on Lara's route underneath.

| Lara's house | Post Office | Town Hall |
|:---:|:---:|:---:|
| to | to | to |
| Post Office | Town Hall | Fairgrounds |
| 3.7 km | 4.5 km | 4.3 km |

**D.** Write and solve a number sentence.

$3.7 + 4.5 + 4.3 = 12.5$

**Answer the question:** Lara travels ___12.5 km___.

## GUIDED PRACTICE

Use the map to answer the questions.

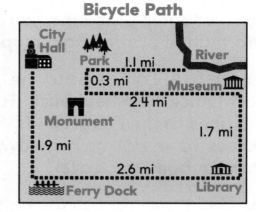

**Bicycle Path**

1. How far is it from City Hall to the ferry dock?

   _____

2. Brian rode from City Hall to the library. Sue rode from the ferry dock to the park. How much farther did Sue ride than Brian?

   **Step 1:** Find out how far each one rode. Write the route and a number sentence for each ride.

   Brian: _____

   _____   Brian rode _____ miles.

   Sue: _____

   _____   Sue rode _____ miles.

   **Step 2:** Subtract to find out how much farther Sue rode.

   _____

   **Answer the question:** Sue rode _____ farther.

3. Sue rode from the monument to the library on Saturday. She rode from the monument to the river on Sunday. How far did she ride in all?

   **Step 1:** Write the routes, then write number sentences.

   _____

   _____

   **Step 2:** Add to find how far she rode in all.

   _____

   **Answer the question:** Sue rode _____.

## PRACTICE

Use the map to answer the questions.

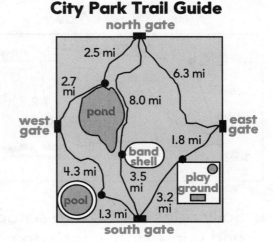

**City Park Trail Guide**

1. Ben came in the west gate and went out the south gate. Ella came in the east gate and went out the south gate. Who walked farther?

   _____

2. How much farther is it from the playground to the band shell than from the playground to the pool?

   _____

3. Caitlin walked from the south gate to the north gate. She passed the band shell. How far did she walk?

   _____

4. Ben started at the north gate. He went out the south gate. What was the shortest route he could take?

   **a.** Compare different routes. Write the places he passed and the distance he walked.

   _____

   _____

   _____

   _____

   _____

   **b.** Which route is shortest?

   _____

# TEST-TAKING PRACTICE

Choose the best answer for each problem.

**Map of Crow Town**

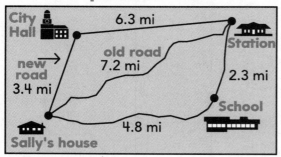

**1.** Sally rides her bike to school and home again each day. **How far does she ride each day?**

A 4.8 miles    C 9.6 miles

B 8 miles      D 16 miles

**2.** Pat walks to City Hall from Sally's house. Then he gets a ride to the station. **How far does he travel in all?**

J 3.4 miles    L 7.2 miles

K 6.3 miles    M 9.7 miles

**3.** Sally can get to the train station from her house on the old road or the new road. **Which route is shorter?**

A 7.2 miles

B the old road

C the new road

D Not given

**4.** The Crow Town race goes from City Hall to the station and then to the school. **Sally ran the whole race. How far did she run?**

J 2 miles      L 6.3 miles

K 2.3 miles    M 8.6 miles

## Write About It

**5.** Describe how you would solve this problem: Jake is going to Sally's house from the station. He can pass the school or pass City Hall or take the old road. He wants to take the shortest route. **Which route should he take?**

_____

_____

1. A☐   B☐   C☐   D☐     3. A☐   B☐   C☐   D☐

2. J☐   K☐   L☐   M☐     4. J☐   K☐   L☐   M☐

● Adding and Subtracting Decimals

# Do You Have Enough Information?

Sometimes the information you need to solve a
problem is not given.

**Example 1:** Liam has $8.75. He wants to buy some
stickers for $3.68 and a sticker book to paste them in.
Does he have enough money?

**A.** Read the problem carefully to find information.
Ask yourself what you know.

**How much money does Liam have?**  _$8.75_

**How much do the stickers cost?**  _$3.68_

**How much does the sticker book cost?**  _Not given_

**B.** Do you have enough information to solve
the problem?

_no_

**Example 2:** Sarah spends $4.62 on a
cookbook. She buys vegetables to make
soup for $8.15. She still has $1.65. How much
money did she start with?

**Step 1:** Read carefully to find information. Ask
yourself what you know.

**How much does the cookbook cost?**  _$4.62_

**How much do the vegetables cost?**  _$8.15_

**How much change does Sarah have?**  _$1.65_

**Step 2:** Do you have enough information?

_yes_

Write and solve a number sentence.

_$4.62 + $8.15 + $1.65 = $14.42_

**Answer the question:** Sarah started with _$14.42_.

© 1999 Metropolitan Teaching & Learning Co.

● Adding and Subtracting Decimals

# GUIDED PRACTICE

1. Barbara gave Tim $5.00 to buy her a soda. He bought the soda for 85¢ and got $4.15 in change. Tim bought a sandwich for himself. How much did he spend at the store?

   **Step 1:** Read carefully to find information.

   Do you know how much Tim spent on soda? _____

   Do you know how much he spent on a sandwich? _____

   **Step 2:** Do you have enough information to solve? _____

   What information do you need?

   _____

2. Linda paid $7.50 for a movie ticket. She has $3.89 left. She wants to buy popcorn for $3.00 and soda for $1.75. Does Linda have enough money?

   **Step 1:** Read carefully to find information. What do you know?

   Do you know how much money Linda has? _____

   Do you know how much popcorn costs? _____

   Do you know how much soda costs? _____

   **Step 2:** Do you have enough information to solve? _____

   **Step 3:** How much money does Linda have? _____

   **Step 4:** Add to find out how much popcorn and soda cost together.

   _____

   **Answer the question:** Does Linda have enough money? _____

## PRACTICE

Find information you need on the sign to solve each problem. If you have enough information, write the answer. If you don't, write what you need to know to solve it.

City Circus
Tickets:
$4 standing room
$5 bleacher seats
$10 front row seats
clown doll: $3.25
pennant: $2.60
light: $5.59

1. Mr. Rosen has a $20 bill. He wants to buy $5 tickets for himself and his children. Does he have enough money?

   _____

2. Abby bought a ticket for a front row seat and a clown doll. She got $4.75 in change. How much money did she start with?

   _____

3. Sam, Max, and Anna were the first people to arrive at the circus. They each bought a bleacher seat. Anna bought a pennant for Max and a light for Sam. How much did Anna spend?

   _____   Anna spent _____

4. KoKo the clown sells cotton candy. She made $27.00 in 3 hours. How many cones of cotton candy did she sell?

   _____

# TEST-TAKING PRACTICE

Choose the best answer for each problem.

**1.** Jim pays $6.50 for a puppet and $3.75 for a toy car. He gets $2.35 in change. Ben buys the same toys. **Who has more money now?**

  **A** Bill has more money.
  **B** You don't have enough information.
  **C** Jim has more money.
  **D** They both spent $10.25.

**2.** Polly knows how much an apple costs. She knows how much money she has. Does she have enough to buy an apple and a sandwich? **What does she need to know?**

  **J** How much money she has.
  **K** How much the sandwich costs.
  **L** How much change she will get.
  **M** All the fruit prices.

**3.** Joyce has $35.00. A one-way bus ticket to the water park costs $9.50. If she buys a ticket there and back, how much money will she have? **Which number sentence shows the problem?**

  **A** $9.50 + $9.50 = $19.00
  **B** $35.00 − $9.50 = $25.50
  **C** $35.00 + $9.50 = $44.50
  **D** Not given

**4.** You know the cost of the toys and the amount of change Cara got. **How can you figure out how much money she started with?**

  **J** Add to find the cost.
  **K** Not enough information.
  **L** Subtract the change from the total.
  **M** Add the cost of the toys to the change.

## Write About It

**5.** Tell how you know if there is enough information to solve this problem: Sam has $6.98. Then he buys 2 yo-yos. Each yo-yo costs $2.75. **How much change does he get? Solve if you have enough information.**

_____

1. A ☐  B ☐  C ☐  D ☐      3. A ☐  B ☐  C ☐  D ☐

2. J ☐  K ☐  L ☐  M ☐      4. J ☐  K ☐  L ☐  M ☐

● Adding and Subtracting Decimals

# Using a Line Graph

A line graph shows change over time.

**Example:** Peg made a graph to show how much money she spent each week.

**Money Spent in October**

**A.** Each horizontal line shows an amount of money.

**What is the greatest amount that can be shown on the graph?**

$ 6.00

**B.** Each point on the graph shows how much Peg spent for 1 week.

Find the point above Week 1. Read across to find the amount.

**How much did Peg spend the first week?** $ 3.00

**C.** Find the highest point on the graph. Read down to find which week it shows. Then read across to find the amount.

**During which week did Peg spend the most money?**

Week 4

**How much did she spend?** $ 4.50

**D.** The lines that connect the points on the graph make it easier to see how the amount Peg spends changes from one week to the next. Write **more** or **less**.

If the line goes up between two points, you know

that Peg spent ___more___.

If the line goes down between two points, you

know that Peg spent ___less___.

● Adding Mixed Numbers

# GUIDED PRACTICE

Use the line graph to answer the questions.

1. How much rain fell in June?

   _____

2. In which month did the most rain fall?

   _____

3. Was there more or less rain in May than in April?

   _____

4. Between what two months did the rainfall increase?

   _____

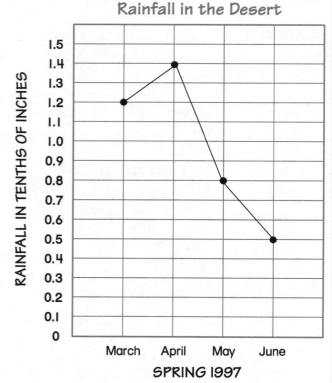

**Rainfall in the Desert**

SPRING 1997

5. How many inches of rain fell in March and April together?

   **Step 1:** Find the information on the graph.

   **rainfall in March:** _____

   **rainfall in April:** _____

   **Step 2:** Add to find how much rain fell in all during those 2 months.

   _____

   **Answer the question:** _____ of rain fell in March and April together.

## PRACTICE
Use the line graph to answer the questions.

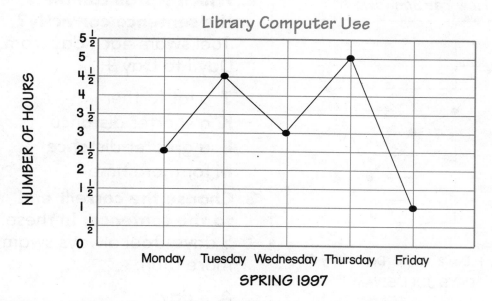

Library Computer Use

NUMBER OF HOURS

Monday  Tuesday  Wednesday  Thursday  Friday

SPRING 1997

1. For how long was the computer used on Thursday? _____

2. On which day was the computer used least? _____

3. Was the computer used for more or less time on

   Wednesday than on Tuesday? _____

4. How long was the computer used on Monday
   and Wednesday together?

   _____  _____ hours

5. How much longer was the computer used on
   Thursday than on Friday?

   _____  _____ longer

6. How long was the computer used during all 5 days?

   _____  _____ hours

• Adding Mixed Numbers

## TEST-TAKING PRACTICE

Choose the best answer for each problem.

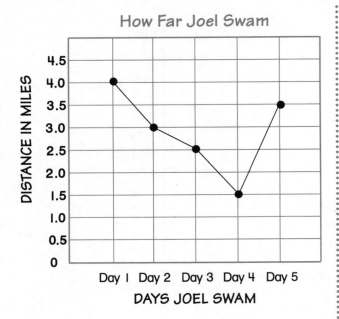

How Far Joel Swam

DISTANCE IN MILES

DAYS JOEL SWAM

**1.** Joel swam laps every day to practice for the race. **On which day did he swim the farthest?**

**A** Day 1
**B** Day 2
**C** Day 3
**D** Day 4

**2. Which words complete the sentence correctly?**
Joel swam each day from Day 1 to Day 4:

**J** a lot farther
**K** a shorter distance
**L** a greater distance
**M** for more time

**3. Choose the correct end to the sentence:** In these 5 days, Joel always swam more than:

**A** 5 days
**B** 3 miles
**C** 1 mile
**D** his brother Abe

**4. How much farther did Joel swim on Day 5 than on Day 4?**

**J** 3.5 miles     **L** 5 miles
**K** 1.5 miles     **M** 2 miles

## Write About It

**5. Explain how you would find out how far Joel swam in 5 days.**

_____

_____

1. A ☐  B ☐  C ☐  D ☐      3. A ☐  B ☐  C ☐  D ☐
2. J ☐  K ☐  L ☐  M ☐      4. J ☐  K ☐  L ☐  M ☐

● Adding Mixed Numbers

# Using a Diagram

You can draw a diagram to help you solve problems that have fractions.

**Example:** Ned has 8 balloons. He gave his sister $\frac{1}{4}$ of his balloons. How many balloons did he give his sister?

**A.** To find $\frac{1}{4}$ of Ned's balloons you have to divide the set of balloons into 4 equal parts. Draw a ring for each part.

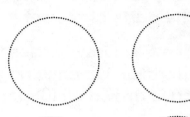

**How many rings do you draw?**

_____4 rings_____

Each ring shows a fraction. What fraction does 1 ring show?

_____$\frac{1}{4}$_____

**What fraction do 3 rings show?** _____$\frac{3}{4}$_____

**B.** Draw a circle to show each balloon. Draw a circle in the first ring. Then, draw a circle in each other ring. Then, start again with a circle in the first ring. Continue until you have drawn 8 circles in all.

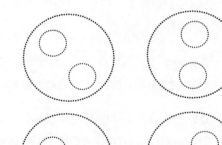

**Is there an equal number of circles in each ring?**

_____yes_____

**How many circles are in each ring?**  _____2 circles_____

**C.** Now you can see how many balloons there are in $\frac{1}{4}$ of 8 balloons.

**Answer the question:** Ned gave his sister _____2 balloons_____.

● Fraction as Part of a Set

**1.** Lars put 18 marbles in his box. Keesha took $\frac{1}{3}$ of the marbles. How many marbles did Keesha take?

**Step 1:** Make 3 rings to show the parts of the set.

**Step 2:** Draw circles to show the marbles, 1 in each ring, until you have drawn all 18 marbles.

**Step 3:** Mark the marbles that Keesha took.

**Answer the question:**

Keesha took _____.

**2.** Peggy picks 20 flowers in the garden. $\frac{1}{5}$ of them are red. What fraction of the flowers are not red?

**Step 1:** Make 5 rings to show the parts of the set.

**Step 2:** Draw circles to show the flowers, until you have drawn all 20 flowers.

**Step 3:** Mark the flowers that are red.

**Answer the question:**

_____ of the flowers are not red.

## PRACTICE
Make a diagram to solve the problem.

1. Sue cuts a string into 10 equal pieces. She uses $\frac{2}{5}$ of the pieces to make a hair tie. How many pieces does she use?

   _____

2. Joe has 14 stickers. He gives Ann $\frac{5}{7}$ of his stickers. How many stickers does he give Ann?

   _____

3. Ann puts 5 stickers on her bulletin board. Of these stickers, $\frac{2}{5}$ glow in the dark. How many stickers do not glow in the dark?

   _____

4. Karl made a pan of cornbread. He cut it into 8 pieces. His father ate 2 pieces and his mother ate 1. What fraction of the cornbread is left?

   _____

5. Peter has 20 shells. Kelly takes $\frac{1}{5}$ of the shells. How many shells are left?

   _____

# TEST-TAKING PRACTICE

Choose the best answer for each problem.

**1.** Jawan has 12 fish. $\frac{1}{4}$ of the fish are silver. **How many fish are silver?**

**A** 3 fish     **C** 8 fish

**B** 4 fish     **D** 9 fish

**2.** The Twirl-a-Ride has 5 cars. There are people in 3 cars. **What fraction of the cars is filled?**

**J** $\frac{1}{5}$     **L** $\frac{3}{5}$

**K** $\frac{1}{3}$     **M** 5 cars

**3.** Helen had 15 stickers. She gave Luis $\frac{1}{3}$ of her stickers. **How many stickers did she keep?**

**A** $\frac{2}{3}$     **C** 5

**B** 2     **D** 10

**4.** Len made 12 brownies. His friends ate 7 brownies. **What fraction of the brownies is left?**

**J** $\frac{1}{12}$     **L** $\frac{7}{12}$

**K** $\frac{5}{12}$     **M** 5 brownies

## Write About It

**5.** Jason has 3 cars. Each car had 4 wheels, but I car lost all its wheels. **What fraction of the wheels are left? Explain how you would make a diagram to show the fraction.**

_____

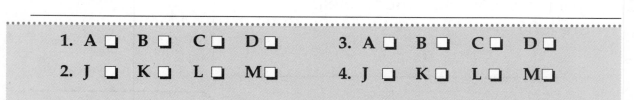

1. A ☐   B ☐   C ☐   D ☐     3. A ☐   B ☐   C ☐   D ☐

2. J ☐   K ☐   L ☐   M ☐     4. J ☐   K ☐   L ☐   M ☐

● Fraction as Part of a Set

# Using a Diagram

You can draw a diagram that shows all the measurements to help you find the perimeter.

**Example 1:** June walks around the swimming pool. The pool is 50 yards long and 25 yards wide. How far does June walk?

**A.** Make a diagram that shows the pool.

The pool is longer than it is wide. **What shape is the pool?** Ring one.

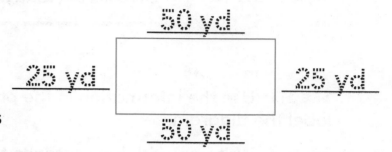

- square
- (rectangle)

**B.** Label each side with the lengths given in the problem.

**C.** To find how far June walks, add the lengths of all 4 sides.

25 + 50 + 25 + 50 = 150

**Answer the question:** June walks __150 yards__.

**Example 2:** Mr. Holtz wants to paint a red line around the bulletin board. The board is 3 feet wide and 3 feet long. How long will the line be?

**Step 1:** Make a diagram. All the sides are the same length. **What shape is the bulletin board?** Ring one.

- (square)
- rectangle

**Step 2:** Add to find the perimeter.

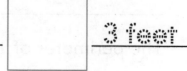

3 + 3 + 3 + 3 = 12

**Answer the question:** The line will be __12 feet__ long.

**I.** Keesha glued a red ribbon around her sign for the street fair. The sign is 36 inches long and 9 inches high. How long is the ribbon?

_____

_____ | Street Fair Today! | _____

_____

**Step 1:** Use the information in the problem to label the diagram.

**Step 2:** Write an addition sentence to find the perimeter.

_____

**Answer the question:** The ribbon is _____ long.

**2.** Ted and Frannie each planted a garden. Ted's garden plot is 4 feet wide and 7 feet long. Frannie's garden is 5 feet long and 5 feet wide. Who needs more fencing?

**Step 1:** Make 2 diagrams and label them with the information in the problem.

**Who has a square garden?** _____

**Step 2:** Write an addition sentence to find the perimeter of each garden.

_____

The perimeter of Ted's garden is _____.

_____

The perimeter of Frannie's garden is _____.

**Answer the question:** _____ needs more fencing.

## PRACTICE
Make a diagram to find the perimeter.

1. Yuri will decorate his picture by putting a border around it with green ribbon. His picture is a rectangle 7 inches tall and 5 inches wide. How long will the ribbon be?

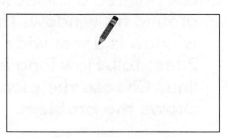

_____    _____

2. Liz makes a daisy chain that she can wrap all the way around the garden shed. The shed is 12 feet by 12 feet. How long is Liz's daisy chain?

_____    _____

3. Carmen gave Will enough ribbon to tape around the edge of the table. If the table is 2 meters wide and 5 meters long, how long is the ribbon?

_____    _____

4. Gary hiked the entire perimeter of the state forest in one week. The forest is 7 miles long and 13 miles wide. How far did Gary hike?

_____    _____

5. Farrah made a triangular flower bed. If all of the sides are 4 feet long, what is the perimeter of the bed?

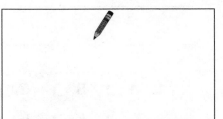

_____    _____

# TEST-TAKING PRACTICE

Choose the best answer for each problem.

**1.** Rick painted a rainbow around his window. The window is 3 feet wide and 2 feet tall. How long is the line? **Choose the picture that shows the problem.**

**A**
2 ft.
3 ft.  3 ft.
2 ft.

**B**
3 ft.
2 ft.  2 ft.
3 ft.

**C**
3 ft.
3 ft.  3 ft.
3 ft.

**D**
2 ft.
2 ft.  3 ft.
3 ft.

**2.** A picture is 16 inches long and 9 inches wide. How long is a ribbon around it? **Which number sentence shows the problem?**

**J** 16 + 9 = 25
**K** 16 + 16 = 32
**L** 16 + 9 + 16 + 9 = 50
**M** 16 + 16 + 16 + 16 = 64

**3.** **How long is the fence around a yard that is 25 feet across and 25 feet from back to front?**

**A** 100 feet       **C** 226 feet
**B** 188 feet       **D** 352 feet

**4.** Patty made a picture with 6 sides. **If each side is 3 inches long, what is the perimeter of the picture?**

**J** 9 inches       **L** 18 inches
**K** 12 inches       **M** 24 inches

## Write About It

**5. Describe the steps you would take to find the perimeter of a playground.**

_____

_____

1. A ☐  B ☐  C ☐  D ☐        3. A ☐  B ☐  C ☐  D ☐
2. J ☐  K ☐  L ☐  M ☐        4. J ☐  K ☐  L ☐  M ☐

● Perimeter

# Finding Area in an Orderly Way

Sometimes you need to find out how
much space a figure covers.

Peter's mask    Nora's mask

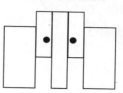 

Peter and Nora each made a mask.
Which mask used more paper?

**A.** Area is a measurement of
how many square units cover the space.

Look at the two masks on dot paper.

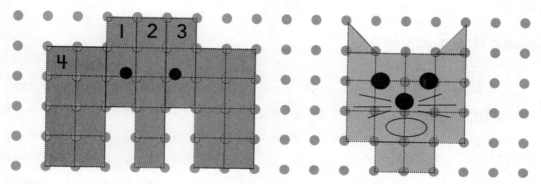

**B.** Draw lines connecting the dots to show the
squares in Peter's mask.

Then number each square. Start at the top on the left
and work across and down. Complete the numbers.

**How many whole squares in Peter's mask?** _27 squares_

**C.** Count the squares in Nora's mask. Number the
whole squares first. Then count the half squares.

**How many whole squares in Nora's mask?** _14 squares_

**How many half squares?**

_2 half squares = 1 square_

**How many squares in all?** _15 squares_

**D. Answer the question:** _Peter's mask_ used more paper.

● Area

## GUIDED PRACTICE

**1.** Jim made these 2 figures.

Which figure covers the most area?

**Step 1:** Draw lines to make squares in the figures.

**Step 2:** Number the squares.

**Answer the question:**

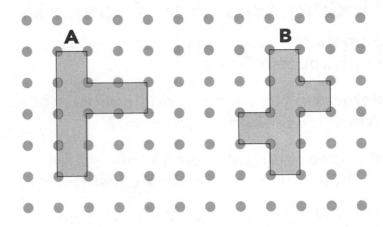

---

**2.** Lee made these figures.

Remember, $\frac{1}{2}$ square △ plus $\frac{1}{2}$ square ▽ equals 1 square □ .

Which of these figures covers the most area?

**Step 1:** Draw lines to make squares in the figures.

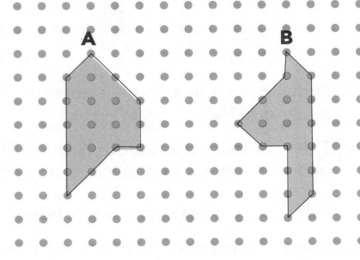

**Step 2:** Number the squares.

How many whole squares in each?  A= _____   B= _____

How many half squares in each?  A= _____   B= _____

**Step 3:** Find the total area of each figure and compare.

A= _____   B= _____

**Answer the question:** Which figure covers the most area?

_____ covers the most area.

## PRACTICE
Draw lines and number squares to find the answers.

**1.** Which figure covers 7 squares?

_____

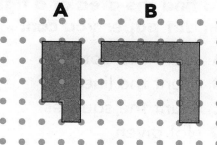

**2.** Which figure covers less area?

S = _____ squares

T = _____ squares

_____ covers less area.

**3.** Which two figures cover the same area?

_____

_____

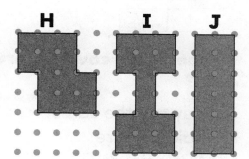

**4.** Which figure covers more than 10 squares?

_____

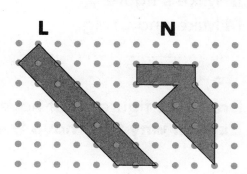

**5.** Draw a figure that has more squares than this one.

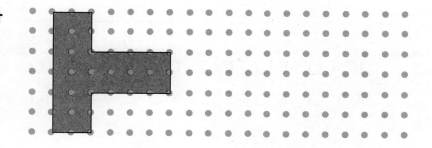

● Area

# TEST-TAKING PRACTICE

Choose the best answer for each problem.

**1. To find the area of a figure on dot paper you can:**

**A** count the dots
**B** count the lines
**C** count the squares
**D** Not given

**2.** Mike made this figure:

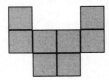

Craig made this one:

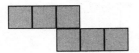

**Whose figure covers more area?**

**J** They are the same.
**K** Craig's figure
**L** Mike's figure
**M** Mike and Craig

**3.** The figure has 5  and

6 ◣ .

**How much area does it cover?**

**A** 5 squares
**B** 8 squares
**C** 11 squares
**D** 17 squares

**4. Which figures cover more than 7 squares?**

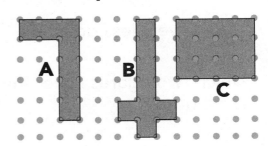

**J** all of them
**K** C and A
**L** A and B
**M** B and C

## Write About It

**5.** Draw two figures that have the same area but different shapes. **Explain why they have the same area.**

_____

_____

1. A ☐  B ☐  C ☐  D ☐      3. A ☐  B ☐  C ☐  D ☐
2. J ☐  K ☐  L ☐  M ☐      4. J ☐  K ☐  L ☐  M ☐

● Area

# Test-Taking Skill: Writing a Plan

Some questions on tests ask you to explain how you solve a problem. You can write a plan to show the steps you take to find the answer.

**Example:** Every month, Lucy put all the pennies she found in a bowl. She showed how many pennies she got each month on a line graph. How many more pennies did she find in May than in the month she found the fewest pennies?

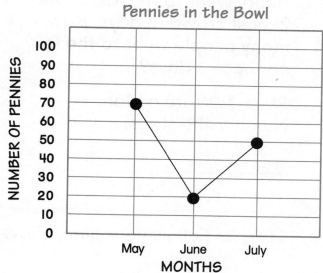

Pennies in the Bowl

**A. To solve this problem you will need to read the line graph.**

**B. Write a plan for finding the answer. Number the steps.**

  **1.** I will find the point on the line graph that shows how many pennies Lucy found in May.

  **2.** Then I will look for the lowest point on the graph to find out in which month Lucy found the fewest pennies.

  **3.** I can subtract that number from the number of pennies Lucy found in May.

**C. Solve by following your plan. Show your calculations.**

  **1.** _____ in May.

  **2.** fewest pennies in _____

  **3.**    $\begin{array}{r} 70 \\ -\ 20 \\ \hline \phantom{00} \end{array}$

**D. Answer the question:** Lucy found _____ more pennies in May than in the month with the fewest pennies.

# TEST-TAKING PRACTICE

Write a plan to solve each problem. Follow the steps of your plan.

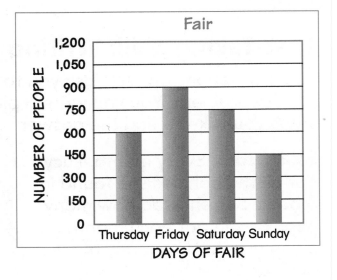

1. Henry went to the fair on the 2 most crowded days. How many people went to the fair on those 2 days?

   **Step 1:** Write a plan. Number the steps.

   _____

   _____

   **Step 2:** Follow your plan. Show your calculations.

   _____

   _____

   **Answer the question:** _____ people went on those 2 days.

2. Did more people come to the fair on Thursday and Friday, or on Saturday and Sunday?

   **Step 1:** Write a plan.

   _____

   _____

   _____

   **Step 2:** Follow your plan. Solve.

   _____

   _____

   _____

   **Answer the question:** More people came _____.

# Underlining Important Information

Sometimes you don't need all of the information given
to solve a problem.

**Example:** Matt's mother works at the Whistle
Factory. She can make 100 whistles in an hour.
She works for 7 hours every day. How many
whistles can she make in 3 hours?

**A.** Ring the question. Underline the
information you need to solve the problem.

- Matt's mother works at the Whistle Factory.

- She can make 100 whistles in an hour.

- She works for 7 hours every day.

- (How many whistles can she make in 3 hours?)

**B.** Multiply to find the answer.

Write a word sentence that shows the problem.
Then write a number sentence.

Hours x Whistles in an hour = Total whistles

3 x 100 = 300

**Answer the question:** She can make 300 whistles
in 3 hours.

**C.** You can answer more than one question about the
same information. Ring the question. Underline the
information you need to answer the question.

- Matt's mother works at the Whistle Factory.

- She can make 100 whistles in an hour.

- She works for 7 hours every day.

- (How many whistles can she make in a day?)

● Multiplication

## GUIDED PRACTICE

**1.** Leo went to the pottery factory.
He learned that 1 potter can
make 20 cups in 1 day. Or,
1 potter can make 40 plates
in 1 day. How many cups can
6 potters make in 1 day?

**Step 1:** Underline the information you need.

**Step 2:** Rewrite the problem as a word sentence.
Then write and solve a number sentence.

_____

_____

**Answer the question:** 6 potters can make

_____ in 1 day.

**2.** A ticket for the movie costs $7 for adults
and $6 for children. There are 300 people in
the club. The club got tickets for 100 children.
How much did they spend for movie tickets?

**Step 1:** Underline the information you need.

**Step 2:** Rewrite the problem as a word sentence
and a number sentence.

_____

_____

**Answer the question:** The club spent _____.

## PRACTICE
Underline the information you need. Then solve.

1. A ticket to a baseball game costs $9 for adults. Students pay only $5. Bob's Sports Club bought 30 adult tickets. How much money did the club pay?

   _____       The club paid _____.

2. A computer factory can make 300 computers per hour. Each worker is paid $15.00 an hour. How many computers can the factory make in 8 hours?

   _____       _____

3. Cupcakes will sell for 50¢ each at the bake sale. Each pan holds 20 cupcakes. If Mary Lynn bakes 5 pans, how many cupcakes will she have to sell?

   _____       _____

4. A fisherman caught the same number of fish every day for a week. He caught 70 fish on the first day. He can sell each fish for $2.00. How many fish in all did he catch on the last three days of that week?

   _____       _____

5. There was a fair for 4 days at the gym. Each day 800 people came to the fair. Raffle tickets were sold at all 6 doors to the gym. The raffle tickets cost $2 each. In all, 700 tickets were sold. How much money did the raffle make?

   _____       The raffle made _____.

# TEST-TAKING PRACTICE

Choose the best answer for each problem.

**1.** There are 4 gates to the fairgrounds. Every hour from 3 o'clock until 6 o'clock, 300 people come in each gate. How many people came in during the first hour? **Choose the number sentence that shows the problem.**

**A** 300 people
**B** 3 x 300 = 900
**C** 4 x 300 = 1,200
**D** 6 x 300 = 1,800

**2.** At the fair, the face painter can paint 50 faces in an hour. The fair is open for 8 hours. **How many faces can the face painter paint in 4 hours?**

**J** 50 faces      **L** 200 faces
**K** 100 faces     **M** 400 faces

**3.** The Kite Club sold kites for $5 each. During the fair they sold 200 kites a day. The fair lasted for 7 days. **How many kites did they sell in all?**

**A** 200 kites
**B** 1,400 kites
**C** 3,500 kites
**D** 7,000 kites

**4.** Tickets cost $6 for adults and $4 for children. During the first hour of the fair 300 tickets were sold to children, and 600 tickets were sold to adults. **How much money did the fair make on the children's tickets?**

**J** $1,200
**K** $1,800
**L** $2,400
**M** $3,600

## Write About It

**5. Explain how you solved problem 3 above. Tell how you decided what information was important.**

_____

_____

| | | |
|---|---|---|
| 1. A ☐  B ☐  C ☐  D ☐ | | 3. A ☐  B ☐  C ☐  D ☐ |
| 2. J ☐  K ☐  L ☐  M ☐ | | 4. J ☐  K ☐  L ☐  M ☐ |

● Multiplication

# Deciding What to Do First

If you have to do more than one operation to solve a problem, start by deciding what to do first.

**Example 1:** A ticket to a football game costs $23. There are 6 people in the Cohen family. Is $100 enough to buy a ticket for all 6 people?

**A. Which is easier to find out?** Ring one.

- ⟨cost of 6 tickets⟩

- whether cost of 6 tickets > $100

**B.** First, multiply to find out how much 6 tickets cost.

_____$6 \times 23 = 138$_____  6 tickets cost ___$138___ .

**C.** Then, compare.

**Is $138 more or less than $100?** ___more___

**Answer the question:** ___no___

**Example 2:** Roger walks the dog 12 blocks each morning and 20 blocks each afternoon. How many blocks do they walk in 7 days?

**Step 1:** Decide which is easier to find out. Ring one.

- ⟨how many blocks each day⟩

- how many blocks in 7 days

**Step 2:** First, add to find out how many blocks they walk each day.

_____$12 + 20 = 32$_____

**Step 3:** Multiply to find how many blocks they walk in 7 days.

_____$7 \times 32 = 224$_____

**Answer the question:** They walk ___224___ blocks in 7 days.

© 1999 Metropolitan Teaching & Learning Co.

## GUIDED PRACTICE

1. Grace wants to buy gifts for each friend who comes to her party. She plans to give each friend 2 mouse stickers and 7 star stickers. She invited 14 people to the party. How many stickers will she need?

**Step 1:** Think about what is easiest to find. Ring what you decide.

- number stickers for all 14 people

- number of stickers per person

**Step 2:** First, add to find out how many stickers for each person.

_____

**Step 3:** Multiply to find out how many stickers for all 14 people.

_____

**Answer the question:** She will need _____ stickers.

2. Paco helps his mother shop. They buy groceries for $89. His mother has five $20 bills. Does she have enough money?

**Step 1:** Decide which to do first, multiply or compare.

**Step 2:** First, multiply to find how much money she has.

_____          She has _____.

**Step 3:** Then compare the cost of the groceries to the amount of money.

_____

**Answer the question:** _____

## PRACTICE

Decide what to do first. Then solve. Show the steps you chose.

1. Jesse rides his bike 8 miles every morning. He rides 12 miles every afternoon. How many miles does he ride in 6 days?

_____   He rides _____.

2. Nicole wants to buy 3 shirts that cost $16 each. She has $40 saved. Can she buy all 3 shirts?

_____   _____

3. The art club spends $25 for an ad and $40 for refreshments each time they hold a show. They had 5 shows last year. How much did they spend all year for shows?

_____   They spent _____.

4. The little theater has 9 rows of chairs. There are 24 chairs in a row. Are there enough chairs if 200 people come to see the play?

_____   _____

5. Tickets for the ice show are $5 for adults and $3 for children. There were 62 adults and 87 children at the show. How much money did the show take in?

_____

The show took in _____.

Choose the best answer for each problem.

**1.** The theater club spends $250 for costumes and $125 for sets for each play. They want to put on 3 plays this year. **How much will they spend?**

**A** $375    **C** $1,125

**B** $750    **D** Not given

**2.** Luke practices piano for 20 minutes in the morning and for 90 minutes in the afternoon. **How many minutes does he practice in 6 days?**

**J** 20 minutes **L** 110 minutes

**K** 90 minutes **M** 660 minutes

**3.** Judy put 8 tops and 16 marbles in each gift box. She made 5 boxes. **How many toys did she use?**

**A** 24 toys    **C** 80 marbles

**B** 40 tops    **D** 120 toys

**4.** Keenan rides the bus to school and home again every day. The bus fare is 45¢ each way. **Is $5 enough for him to pay the bus fare for 5 days?**

**J** yes

**K** not enough

**L** no

**M** $4.50

## Write About It

**5.** A ticket to the concert costs $15 for adults and $8 dollars for children. If 2 adults and 3 children are going together, how much will they pay in all?

**Explain how you would solve this problem. Tell why you choose to do one step before another.**

_____

_____

_____

1. A ☐  B ☐  C ☐  D ☐      3. A ☐  B ☐  C ☐  D ☐

2. J ☐  K ☐  L ☐  M ☐      4. J ☐  K ☐  L ☐  M ☐

● Multiplying by 1-Digit Numbers

# Drawing a Diagram to Understand Remainders

Sometimes when you divide a number into equal groups, you get a remainder, or a part of a group, left over. To solve the problem you need to think about what the remainder means.

**Example 1:** There are 23 people going to the fair. A car can hold 5 people. How many cars do they need?

**A.** Write the division problem. You can show the problem by making a diagram.

$$\begin{array}{r} 4\text{ R }3 \\ 5\overline{)23} \\ -\underline{20} \\ 3 \end{array}$$

   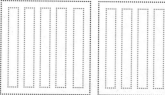 

**B.** Look at the answer. Decide what to do with the remainder.

**THINK:** They will need another car to take the 3 people left over. So, it makes sense to round the quotient up to 5.

**Answer the question:** They need _5 cars_.

**Example 2:** Ben packs 5 ripe tomatoes in each basket. There are 23 ripe tomatoes in the crate. How many baskets can he pack?

**Step 1:** Write the problem. The division is the same as in Example I.

**Step 2.** Look at the answer. Decide what to do with the remainder.

**THINK:** There are 3 ripe tomatoes left over. Ben can't put fewer than 5 in a basket, so, it makes sense to round down the quotient to 4.

**Answer the question:** Ben packs _4 baskets_.

● Dividing with Remainders

## GUIDED PRACTICE

Divide to solve each problem. Decide what to do with
the remainder.

1. The clown has 23 balloons. There are 5 children at the
   party. Each child gets the same number of balloons.
   How many balloons does the clown give each child?

   **Step 1:** Complete the diagram to show the problem.

   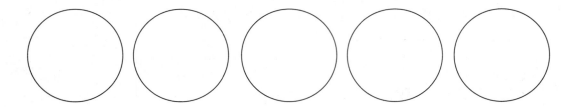

   Write the problem and divide.

   **Step 2:** Round up or down. Check one.

   ___ Round up. The clown can give more balloons to
   some children.

   ___ Round down. The clown gives each child the
   same number of balloons.

   **Answer the question:** The clown gives each child _____.

2. Alan has 44 photos. He always puts the same
   number of photos on each page of his albums.
   If an album has 6 pages, how many photos does
   he put on each page?

   **Step 1:** Draw a diagram. Write the problem and divide.

   **Step 2:** Decide what to do with the remainder.

   **Answer the question:** He puts _____ on each page.

## PRACTICE

Write each problem. Solve. Decide what to do with the remainder.

**1.** The school has 34 baseballs. There are 4 teams. How many baseballs can the coach give each team so they have the same number of balls?

Each team can have _____.

**2.** Lisa's dad baked 20 cookies. He puts 3 cookies in each bag. How many bags does he need if all the cookies go in bags?

He needs _____.

**3.** Each picnic table seats 6 people. A group of 25 people is eating lunch. How many picnic tables does the group need?

The group needs _____.

**4.** The bus holds 10 people. There are 35 students taking the field trip. How many buses do they need?

The students need _____.

**5.** Luis has 34 marbles. He gives 5 friends each 6 marbles. How many marbles does he have left?

Luis has _____ left.

## TEST-TAKING PRACTICE

Choose the best answer for each problem.

**1.** Each table in the restaurant has 4 chairs. A group of 22 people comes in. **How many tables do they need?**

**A** 4      **C** 6
**B** 5      **D** 7

**2.** The teacher has 24 pencils. There are 9 students. Each student gets the same number of pencils. **How many pencils will each student get?**

**J** 2      **L** 9
**K** 3      **M** 24

**3.** Sarah has 15 stickers. She wants to put 4 stickers on each page of her book. **How many pages does she use?**

**A** 3      **C** 6
**B** 4      **D** 15

**4.** Ms. Daikers has 28 peaches. She puts 6 in a bag. **How many bags does she need to put all of them in bags?**

**J** 2      **L** 4
**K** 3      **M** 5

### Write About It

**5.** Make a plan to solve this problem. Explain how you decide what to do with the remainder.

Tina is giving a party. She bakes 20 cupcakes. There are 9 guests. **How many cupcakes can each guest have if all guests have the same number of cupcakes?**

_____

_____

_____

1. A☐ B☐ C☐ D☐     3. A☐ B☐ C☐ D☐
2. J☐ K☐ L☐ M☐     4. J☐ K☐ L☐ M☐

●Dividing with Remainders

# Underlining Important Information

Sometimes you don't need all of the information given to solve a problem. Start by reading the whole problem and deciding which information you need.

**Example:** The baker has an order for 240 muffins and 32 cakes. Each pan holds 8 muffins. How many pans of muffins must she bake?

**A.** Ring the question. Underline the information you need to solve the problem.

The baker has an order for 240 muffins and 32 cakes. Each pan holds 8 muffins.

(How many pans of muffins must she bake?)

**B.** Write a word sentence that shows the problem.

Total muffins ÷ Muffins in 1 pan = Number of pans

**C.** Write and solve a number sentence.

240 ÷ 8 = 30

**Answer the question:**

She must bake ___30 pans___ of muffins.

1. There are 4 basketball leagues in River County. Each basketball team in the county has 9 players. If there are 270 players, how many teams are there?

   **Step 1:** Read the problem. Underline the information you need.

   **Step 2:** Rewrite the problem as a word sentence. Then write and solve a number sentence.

   _____

   _____

   **Answer the question:** There are _____.

2. A swim meet has 8 relay races. The 4 swimmers in one relay race swim 200 meters in all. How many meters does each person swim?

   **Step 1:** Read the problem. Underline the information you need.

   **Step 2:** Rewrite the problem as a word sentence. Then write and solve a number sentence.

   _____

   _____

   **Answer the question:** Each person swims _____.

## PRACTICE
Read carefully. Underline the information you need.
Then solve.

1. About 350 students buy lunch each day. Today, there are 360 students buying lunch. Each can of fruit serves 9 students. How many cans of fruit does the cafeteria need today?

   _____  The cafeteria needs _____ cans.

2. Jim worked 4 days last week and 5 days this week. He made $250 this week. How much did he earn each day?

   _____  Jim earned _____ each day.

3. Each barn holds 9 horses or 12 cows. The farm has 180 horses. How many barns are there?

   _____  There are _____ barns.

4. The pet store has 4 tanks of small fish and 3 tanks of large fish. There are 160 small fish. How many small fish are in each tank?

   _____  There are _____ small fish in each tank.

5. Each load of laundry takes 7 quarters. Gina puts 4 quarters in the washer and 3 in the dryer. Gina has 140 quarters. How many loads of laundry can she do?

   _____  Gina can do _____ loads of laundry.

6. A tree farmer has 480 apple trees and 350 pine trees. He will plant the apple trees in rows of 8 each, and the pine trees in rows of 7 each. How many rows of apple trees will he have?

   _____  He will plant _____ rows of apple trees.

Choose the best answer for each problem.

**1.** Theo has 540 lettuce plants and 50 tomato plants. He will plant 6 rows of lettuce. How many plants will each row have? **Choose the sentence that shows the problem.**

**A** 540 ÷ 50     **C** 50 ÷ 6

**B** 540 ÷ 6     **D** 6 x 50

**2.** Maria made $360 last week and $350 the week before. **If she worked 4 days last week, how much money did she make each day?**

**J** $9     **L** $90

**K** $40     **M** $99

**3.** Each vest has 6 buttons. Mr. Taylor has 420 buttons and 900 yards of ribbon. **How many vests can he make?**

**A** 7 vests     **C** 300 vests

**B** 70 vests     **D** 700 vests

**4.** Matt, John, and Helen have 900 sports cards. They have 420 baseball cards and 480 basketball cards. **If they want to split all of the cards evenly among them, how many cards will each one get?**

**J** 140 cards     **L** 300 cards

**K** 160 cards     **M** Not given

## Write About It

**5.** Peters Pickles packs 5 pickles in each small sack and 10 pickles in each large sack.  They sold 250 pickles on Saturday. They only sold small sacks. How many small sacks did they sell? **Explain how you would solve this problem.**

_____

_____

_____

_____

1. A ☐  B ☐  C ☐  D ☐     3. A ☐  B ☐  C ☐  D ☐

2. J ☐  K ☐  L ☐  M ☐     4. J ☐  K ☐  L ☐  M ☐

# Choosing the Operation to Do First

You might have to do more than one operation to solve some problems. Decide what to do first.

**Example 1:** The science center has 8 chairs in a row. Mrs. Teng's class has 28 students. Both Ms. Rizzo's class and Mr. Kent's class have 34 students. How many rows will the 3 classes fill?

**A.** **Which is easier to do? Check one.**

___ find the total number of students, and then divide

___ find the number of rows for each class, then add

**B.** Try adding first. Write the problem and solve.

___34 + 34 + 28 = 96___   **Total:** __96 students__.

**C.** Now, divide the total number of students by the number of chairs in a row to find the number of rows.

__96 ÷ 8 = 12__

**Answer the question:** The 3 classes fill __12 rows__.

**Example 2:** Paco can buy 8 bags of oranges for $32 at Bob's or 6 bags of oranges for $30 at Supermart. Which store has the better price?

**Step 1:** **Decide what to do first.**

**Step 2:** First, find the price of 1 bag of oranges.

| Bob's | Supermart |
|---|---|
| 32 ÷ 8 = 4 | 30 ÷ 6 = 5 |
| __$4__ a bag. | __$5__ a bag. |

**Step 3:** Now, compare the cost. ___$4 < $5___

**Answer the question:** __Bob's__ has the better price.

## GUIDED PRACTICE

**1.** Sue is making a mosaic with tiles. She has 26 red tiles and 10 black tiles to put in rows. Each row will hold 9 tiles. How many rows will she fill?

**Step 1:** Think about what you need to know first. Check the easier problem.

___ number of rows of red and black tiles

___ number of tiles Sue has in all

**Step 2:** First, add to find out how many tiles Sue has in all.

_____      Sue has _____ tiles.

**Step 3:** Divide the total number of tiles by the number of tiles in each row to find the number of rows.

_____

**Answer the question:** Sue will fill _____ rows.

**2.** Mario can buy 2 bags of pears from Bob's for $12 or 3 bags of pears from Supermart for $15. Which store has the better price?

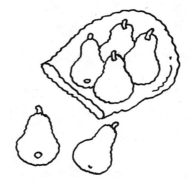

**Step 1:** Decide what to do first.

**Step 2:** Divide the price by the number of bags to find how much each bag costs.

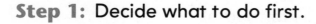

_____      _____

**Step 3:** Then compare the cost.

Bob's pears cost _____ a bag.

Supermart's pears cost _____ a bag.

**Answer the question:** _____ has the better price.

## PRACTICE

Decide what to do first. Then solve. Show the steps you chose.

1. A teacher can buy 9 cases of pencils for $117 or 7 cases of pencils for $105. Which is the better buy?

   _____        _____

   _____

   The better buy is _____.

2. A gardener plants 9 lettuce plants in each row. He has 45 plants of red lettuce and 36 plants of green lettuce. How many rows of lettuce does he plant?

   _____

   _____        He plants _____.

3. Mara and Karl each have 160 stickers. Mara puts 8 stickers on each page of her book. Then Karl puts 4 stickers on each page of his book. How many pages have stickers in both books?

   _____

   _____        They use _____ in both books.

4. Keesha has 53 red beads and 85 blue beads. She wants to make necklaces to sell at the fair. If she puts 6 beads on each necklace, how many can she make?

   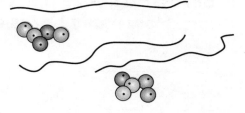

   _____

   _____        She can make _____.

# TEST-TAKING PRACTICE

Choose the best answer for each problem.

**1.** Max makes a mosaic with 8 tiles in each row. He has 32 red tiles and 40 green tiles. How many rows does he make? **Which number sentence shows the best first step?**

**A** 32 + 40 = 72
**B** 32 ÷ 8 = 4
**C** 72 ÷ 8 = 9
**D** 40 − 32 = 22

**2.** There are 34 science books and 47 storybooks in the library return box. The librarian carries 9 books at a time. **How many trips does she take to carry all of the books to the desk?**

**J** 81 books     **L** 9 trips
**K** 9 books      **M** Not given

**3.** The Little Theater has 7 chairs in each row. There are 25 people who have bought tickets. Another 24 people are on line to buy tickets. **How many rows of chairs will all of them fill?**

**A** 3 rows     **C** 7 rows
**B** 4 rows     **D** 49 chairs

**4.** Bob's sells 6 bags of corn for $54. Supermart sells 9 bags of corn for $72. Which is the best buy? **Which operation would be the best first step?**

**J** divide to find the cost of 1 bag from each store
**K** add $54 + $72
**L** subtract $54 from $72
**M** compare the number of bags sold

## Write About It

**5.** Write a plan for how to solve this problem: Yuri puts his toy cars in boxes. He has 23 black cars and 33 red cars. Each box holds 8 cars. **How many boxes does he need?**

_____

_____

_____

1. A☐  B☐  C☐  D☐     3. A☐  B☐  C☐  D☐
2. J☐  K☐  L☐  M☐     4. J☐  K☐  L☐  M☐

# Using a Table

To solve some problems, you have to find information on a table. Then you have to decide what kind of answer you need.

**Example 1:** Jim packs 9 marbles in each bag. How many bags can he pack?

| Item | Number in Stock | Price for 1 Set |
|------|-----------------|-----------------|
| marbles | 297 | $3.60 |
| jacks | 540 | $1.32 |

**A.** Find the information you need in the table.

**How many marbles are there in all?** _297_

**B.** Decide what kind of answer you will get. Check one.

___ number    ___ money

Decide what to do to find the answer. Check one.

___ multiply    ___ divide

**C.** Write and solve the division problem. _297 ÷ 9 = 33_

**Answer the question:** Jim can pack _33_ bags of marbles.

**Example 2:** Paul sells 5 packs of jacks. How much money does he get?

**Step 1:** Find the information you need in the table.

**How much does 1 pack of jacks cost?** _$1.32_

**Step 2:** Decide what kind of answer you will get.

Decide what to do to find the answer. Check one.

___ multiply    ___ divide

Write and solve the multiplication problem.

_1.32 x 5 = 6.60_

**Answer the question:** Paul gets _$6.60_.

● Multiplication and Division with 1-Digit Numbers

# GUIDED PRACTICE

Find the information you need on the table. Then decide what kind of answer you need and solve.

1. The breakfast tables at Sally's Diner are set for 7 people. How many people ate breakfast there on May 1?

| Sally's Diner – May 1 | | |
|---|---|---|
| Meal | Group Rate | Tables Filled |
| Breakfast | $15.25 | 34 |
| Lunch | $27.36 | 13 |

**Step 1:** Find the information you need on the table. Choose the kind of answer.

___ money    ___ number

Choose the operation.

___ divide    ___ multiply

**Step 2:** Write and solve the problem. _____

**Answer the question:** _____ people ate breakfast.

2. A group of 9 friends ate lunch. They each paid an equal share of the meal. How much did each person pay?

**Step 1:** Find the information you need on the table.

Choose the kind of answer.

___ money    ___ number

Choose the operation.

___ divide    ___ multiply

**Step 2:** Write and solve the problem. _____

**Answer the question:** Each person paid _____.

## PRACTICE

Use the table to help you solve the problems.

I. Groups of 10 adults can go to
Science Island for the special
rate. How much does each
person pay?

_____

_____

| Science Island Group Rates | | |
|---|---|---|
| Type of Ticket | Tickets Sold this Week | Cost per Group |
| adult | 314 | $13.50 |
| student | 76 | $12.50 |
| under 12 years | 432 | $7.20 |
| over 65 years | 58 | $9.75 |

2. Children under 12 come most
often to Science Island. There
are 8 children in each group.
How many groups came this week?

_____          _____

3. Each child in a group of 8 pays an equal share of
the group rate. How much does each child pay?

_____          _____

4. Mount Jerome School sent 4 groups of students.
There were 12 students in each group. How much
did the school pay in all?

_____          _____

5. The same number of people over age 65 came for
3 weeks in a row. How many came in all?

_____          _____

● Multiplication and Division by 1-Digit Numbers

# TEST-TAKING PRACTICE

Choose the best answer for each problem.

| fruit | number picked | basket price |
|-------|---------------|--------------|
| apples | 972 | $3.45 |
| pears | 855 | $6.75 |

**I.** The Chorus picked fruit to sell at the street fair. They put 12 apples in each basket. **How many kinds of fruit did they pick?**

**A** 2      **C** 972

**B** 12      **D** 1,827

**2.** Each basket gets 12 apples. **How many baskets of apples did they pack?**

**J** 12      **L** 108

**K** 81      **M** $41.40

**3.** Each basket gets 12 apples. **Choose the sentence that shows how much each apple cost.**

**A** $3.45 ÷ 12

**B** $6.75 ÷ 12

**C** 12 x $3.45

**D** 972 x $3.45

**4.** The Chorus packed 9 pears in each basket. **To find out how many baskets they packed with pears, you would:**

**J** multiply 9 times the number of pears picked.

**K** subtract the number of pears from the number of apples.

**L** divide the cost of a basket by the number of pears.

**M** divide the number of pears picked by 9.

## Write About It

**5.** Describe your plan for solving this problem. The Chorus sold 27 baskets of apples the first day of the fair. **How much money did they make?**

_____

_____

_____

1. A ☐  B ☐  C ☐  D ☐     3. A ☐  B ☐  C ☐  D ☐

2. J ☐  K ☐  L ☐  M ☐     4. J ☐  K ☐  L ☐  M ☐

© 1999 Metropolitan Teaching & Learning Co.

● Multiplication and Division by 1-Digit Numbers

# Test-Taking Skill: **Try Out the Answer Choices**

You might have trouble finding the answer on a multiple-choice test. First, decide what kind of answer you want. Then, try out the different answer choices to find the correct answer.

**Example:** Jake has 7 bags of marbles. Alison has 2 bags of marbles. Each bag has 32 marbles. How many marbles do they have together?

**A** 9 bags   **B** 14 marbles   **C** 224 marbles   **D** 288 marbles

**A.** **Decide what kind of answer you want.** The answer will be the number of marbles Jake and Alison have together.

**B.** **Try each answer choice. Ask yourself if it can be the right answer.**

**Choice A:** *THINK:* No, the question asks for the number of marbles, not the number of bags.

**Choice B:** *THINK:* No, 14 is 7 x 2. You can't find the number of marbles by multiplying the number of bags by each other.

**Choice C:** *THINK:* No, 7 x 32 = 224. That only tells you how many marbles Jake has.

**Choice D:** *THINK:* The answer must be D. You can get this number this way.

Add the number of bags Jake has to the number of bags Alison has to find out how many they have together. Then multiply by 7 to find out how many marbles they have in all.

**C.** **Mark the answer form.**

© 1999 Metropolitan Teaching and Learning Co.

1. A❑  B❑  C❑  D❑

# TEST-TAKING PRACTICE

Try out the different answer choices, then choose the best answer and mark the box with the same letter.

I. Clark reads 15 pages in his science book every day. The book is 450 pages long. How many days will it take to read the whole book?

**A** 15 pages     **C** 30 days

**B** 3 days      **D** 300 days

**Step 1: Decide what kind of answer you want.**

**Step 2: Try out the answer choices. Write your reasons for deciding an answer choice is wrong.**

**Choice A:** _____

_____

**Choice B:** _____

_____

**Choice C:** _____

_____

**Choice D:** _____

_____

**Step 3:** Choose the correct letter and fill in the box below.

2. Elsa can make 2 batches of cookies in an hour. How many batches can she mix if she bakes for 3 hours every day for 6 days?

**J** 6 batches     **L** 18 hours

**K** 11 batches    **M** 36 batches

1. A ☐   B ☐   C ☐   D ☐    2. J ☐   K ☐   L ☐   M ☐